THE COMPLETE JACK RUSSELL TERRIER

THE COMPLETE
JACK RUSSELL TERRIER

David Brian Plummer

Photographs by Keith Ruston

The Boydell Press

© 1980 D. B. Plummer

First published 1980 by The Boydell Press
an imprint of Boydell & Brewer Ltd
PO Box 9, Woodbridge, Suffolk IP12 3DF

Reprinted 1986, 1987

British Library Cataloguing in Publication Data

Plummer, David Brian
    The complete Jack Russell terrier.
    1. Jack Russell terrier
    I. Title
    636.7′55   SF429.J27

ISBN 0-85115-121-3

Printed and bound in Great Britain at
The Camelot Press Ltd, Southampton

CONTENTS

ILLUSTRATIONS

15. A fox drawn alive and unharmed.
16. A tremendous day's hunting using terriers and a lurcher.
17. Fox bites invariably cause massive facial swellings.
18. A badger skull is hinged and it is nearly impossible for the jaw to dislocate.
19. A permit is required before a hunter is allowed to dig badger.
20. A badger set that is obviously in use. Note the striations caused by the badgers' claws.
21. A 'scratch' tree – a sure sign an established badger colony is nearby.
22. The almost legendary Brough's Earths – probably the largest badger set in the world. Over the centuries over a thousand tons of earth have been excavated by badgers.
23. A deceptive 'one eye' set. This earth has been the burial ground of many terriers.
24. A delving rod is a priceless tool to ascertain the depth of an earth.
25. Trenching through to the sound of the baying: the start of a badger dig.
26. A badger is tailed at the end of a dig.
27. End of the dig – a badger's ursine head appears at the end of the excavation.
28. A badger, alive and unharmed, is crated and transported to a new home.
29. Badger bites are quite distinct from the wounds inflicted by foxes and are usually 'pincer-like' nips inflicted on the lower jaw and neck of the dog.
30. The real Scottish wildcat – a fearsome foe for any terrier.
31. A rabbit bolt hole: practically invisible to the human eye, but easily detected by the first class rabbiting terrier.
32. An even, level litter: the hall mark of the true-breeding strain.
33. Sparrow suggests that a bull terrier cross should be used periodically to improve head size.
34. A powerful jaw is a prime requisite of a working terrier: the author's champion Warlock.
35. A correct scissor bite. See standard of excellence for the Jack Russell Terrier.

INTRODUCTION

Man is a baffling creature. At the time of writing, the two most popular breeds of dog in the country are the lurcher and the Jack Russell terrier, both plebeian breeds, both breeds owned and worked by artisan hunters, both breeds unregistered and untouched by the edicts of the Kennel Club. Yet, strangely, these breeds are now becoming curious status symbols. The Jack Russell terrier – really a mongrelly little beast, if the truth be told – is now in the hands of those who claim that the breed has great antiquity, and each and every Jack Russell terrier would now appear to be descended from the dogs of the West Country parson who gave his name to the breed.

It is the writer's wish that, if this book does little else, it will destroy such foolish mythology and give at least an insight into the history, psychology and working abilities of a dog who should never become a show-bred piece of uselessness, but should remain the useful little hunter and all-round worker it is today. Twenty years from now, perhaps the combination of the show craze and the public disdain for field sports will have allowed this game little dog to degenerate into a lap dog, an old lady's companion. Indeed, it almost certainly will become quite simply a pet. If this should come to pass, let this book then be seen as a historical curio, a relic of the time when the Jack Russell terrier was one of the most useful and popular working dogs. But, above all, let us pray that my premonition of the future, of a time when man is denied his right to hunt and to train his hunting dogs, is incorrect and unduly pessimistic.

Enough, however, of guesswork, premonition and hypotheses. As they say in the story synopses in ladies' magazines, 'Now read on . . .'

1 THE LEGEND

It is said that Parson John Russell, Vicar of Swimbridge in Devon, acquired his first terrier while studying at Oxford. The dates of this supposed acquisition vary between 1815 and 1819, and story has it that John Russell purchased his first terrier from a milkman, supposedly in the village of Marston in Oxfordshire. Russell's purchase – a type of fox terrier – was said to be roughly fourteen inches at the shoulder, rough of coat and predominantly white, approximating in size to a fully grown vixen. Story further has it that this terrier, a bitch called Thump, was to be the ancestor of all of the parson's virtually legendary strain of terriers. What the parson used to 'cover' this terrier to produce his strain is open to speculation, and frankly of no importance to the modern Jack Russell breeder. Sufficient to say that, by the 1850s, Parson John Russell was one of the leading breeder/dealers of fox terriers in the West Country.

Russell was an almost obsessional hunter and stories are legion concerning his expulsion from schools on account of his predatory menagerie of ferrets, terriers and hounds which were his lifelong pets and companions. When he eventually obtained a position as curate of George Nympton, he quickly set about putting together a pack of hounds and hunted firstly otter, spending his winters assisting another hunting parson, the Reverend Jack Froude of Knowstone, in the pursuit of fox.

To the reader, used as he is to the *Punch* caricatures of parsons, meek of disposition and bland and boring, as many of the clergy are forced to be by circumstance, the image of a rural parson riding to hounds like a country squire may seem a little bizarre. A mere glance at the history of the West Country during the nineteenth century would, however, convince the reader that Russell, the sporting, hunting, shooting, fishing parson, was by no means an exception in the Devonshire of the Victorian era. Time seemed to have stood still in Devonshire and characters more at home in the climes of a century earlier still abounded there – bizarre, eccentric and near lunatic characters were common enough in the West Country. Among Russell's close associates was Templer of Stowe, a cultured, witty man who rode to hounds with a monkey strapped to the saddle of a horse and shot rabbits over a mixed pack of foxes and terriers. Froude, the Vicar of Knowstone, ran a gang of disreputables who terrorized the villages near his parish, burning, stealing and looting according to whatever took their fancies.

Even these roughnecks were dwarfed by another, the awesome Jack Radford, Vicar of Lapworth, whom Russell almost certainly must have known about, if not known personally. Radford was an amazing villain – a veritable giant of a man whom Drake, in his *A North Devon Village*, describes as having a 54-inch chest with arms like oak saplings. Radford spent little time in the pew, but was noted for his skill at wrestling and for showing savage violence towards anyone who offended him. It was said that he spent a great deal of his time around the gipsy and tinker encampments which infested Devonshire at this time, wrestling anyone who was witless enough to challenge the giant. So fascinating were these villainous parsons, more at home in a London rookery than a sleepy Devonshire village, that R. D. Blackmore, author of *Lorna Doone*, used Froude and Radford as models for his ferocious and infamous characters, the Reverend Chowne and Rambone, in his little-known but highly readable book, *The Maid of Sker*. Clearly Russell would not have seemed at all an odd-man-out in the social climate of his times.

Russell used his terriers to flush quarry for his hounds, and he was quite insistent that the terriers should not be required to thrash a fox, cripple or kill it, but were to nip and tease the fox to persuade him that he would be better occupied above ground than battling in the Stygian darkness of the earth. The great fad during the nineteenth century was to cross the various terriers of Britain with bulldogs to produce an extraordinary tough and hard terrier, but Russell disapproved of this since the inclusion of bulldog blood ruined what Russell called 'the gentlemanly characteristics' of his strain. He is reputed to have preferred rough-coated terriers, as most of the smooth fox terriers of the time had bulldog blood in their ancestry. Perhaps it is true that he did prefer rough-coated terriers but he certainly also bred many smooth-coated dogs at his kennels in Swimbridge. Few of Russell's fox terriers were docked or had cropped ears, and the undocked squirrel tails that characterized his terriers were sometimes regarded with distaste by his fellow hunters. Russell, however, insisted that the natural undocked tail enabled him to be able to grip the terrier by its stern and draw the beast from an earth whenever it had latched on to its foe.

Whether or not John Russell kept a strain of rough-coated fox terriers will continue to be debated for years to come. Many accuse the parson of having been simply a dealer, buying and breeding from any terrier that took his fancy, supplementing his meagre income by wheeling and dealing in livestock. One thing is fairly certain, however:

that he did much to popularize the wire-haired fox terrier – now one of the most popular breeds in Britain, but at that time a Cinderella, a poor relation of the smooth fox terrier. Russell was, in fact, one of the founder members of the Kennel Club.

Russell died in 1883, and his kennels were dispersed, some reputedly passing to Squire Nicholas Snow of Oare. These became the foundation stock of one Arthur Heinemann, who is often cited as the last of the breeders of the true Jack Russell terrier. If Russell was a bizarre character, Heinemann was even more of one, and in addition to using his terriers to both fox and otter (he was Master of Hounds at Cheriton), he used his team to dig badger. Heinemann died in 1930, after reputedly squandering a fortune of £70,000, and his strain of terrier was dispersed literally to the winds. From time to time, however, one sees advertisements for 'genuine' Jack Russell terriers, always descended from Jack Russell's dogs through Heinemann's illustrious Lynton Jack. The reader would do well always to treat such claims with a pinch of salt – I recommend a block or two.

Let us now consider the logic, indeed the mathematics, behind any claim that a dog could be a genuine Jack Russell terrier. Russell died in 1883, roughly a hundred years ago, so unless chronic inbreeding was practised by anyone who purchased dogs from the parson – inbreeding which could only have had a detrimental effect on the constitution of the progeny – the original bloodline would have become highly diluted by outcrosses with other strains. Furthermore, few working-terrier breeders keep anything like accurate pedigrees. Joan Begbie, whose Seale Cottage strain of Jack Russell was reputedly bred from the dogs of John Russell, kept accurate pedigrees tracing her terrier bloodlines back to Nimrod Capel's 'Bluecap', a dog supposedly bred from John Russell's strain of fox terrier, but, again, it must be said that Miss Begbie also used John Cobby's (Huntsman for the South-West Wiltshire) strain for repeated outcross, and while Cobby certainly kept accurate pedigrees and had excellent working terriers, he never once claimed that his hunt terriers were descended from the dogs of John Russell.

Frankly, the dogs of John Russell had little or no influence on the evolution of the modern Jack Russell terrier. In time, for want of a name, any white-bodied working terrier of dubious ancestry simply came to be known as a Jack Russell, and dogs with obvious Sealy-ham, fox-terrier and even Lakeland terrier ancestry are often seen at Jack Russell terrier shows. These dogs are no worse for having mixed blood, not a whit inferior for their dubious ancestry. Most modern Jack Russell terriers will, if given a chance, work just as well as did the dogs of both Russell and Heinemann.

The Fact behind the Legend

Having decided that the present-day white-bodied hunt terrier is not, or at the most only slightly, connected with the dogs of the Reverend John Russell, what are the dogs that we today call, for want of a better term, Jack Russell terriers? Well, the reader must first dispense with the notion sadly perpetuated in a great number of books that God created John Russell and terriers came into being. For as long as man has been plagued with 'earth-living' or 'set-living' types of vermin, there have been terriers bred to cope with them. We know for certain that, during the sixth century, terriers were given as a gift by one Germanic king to another, and it is likely that Britain also had dogs capable of going to ground at subterranean quarry even before this date.

As to the shape, type and colour coat of those early terriers, it is a matter of pure speculation – educated guesswork at best. Only one thing is certain, that these terriers were small enough to get to ground to fox or badger; otherwise they would not have been considered earth dogs – which, incidentally, is what the word 'terrier' means, derived as it is from the Latin *terra*, the earth. As to colour and coat, we might, at the risk of being a little unscientific, hazard a guess. Most early prints and illustrations which show terriers – including those of the earth-stopper depicted in Sparrow's delightful book, *The Terrier Vocation* – resembled mongrels 'twixt Cairn and terrier, undocked and rough and ragged of coat. The reader should now immediately dispense with the notion that these terriers were in any way standardized like the terriers of today. Travel was difficult and slow, so each district tended to breed its own kind of terrier – many of which were the ancestors of such breeds as the Norwich, the Norfolk, the Cairn, the Bedlington and so forth. These native British terriers did, in fact, live hard lives, perched as they were on the lowest rung of the canine ladder, while few, if any, were bred for good looks. Hence game dogs were bred to game dogs with scarcely a care being paid to the appearance of either parent.

Prior to 1700, few white-bodied dogs were to be found among the native British terriers, partly because few white-bodied puppies appeared in terrier litters, and partly because white pigmentation was regarded with suspicion by the British hunter of a few centuries ago. This idea still prevails in the North, where white coloration is often regarded as indicating constitutional weakness. Border terriers with white feet are still disqualified in the show ring, and whites born in a litter of Cairn terriers used to be put to death since they were judged to have all manner of maladies, ranging from deafness to sterility. To be fair, there was a certain element of truth in these fears. By 1880, many strains of fighting bulldog – a breed which was frequently white or pied – had become so inbred as a result of fanciers and dog fighters jealously guarding their strains of bulldog and mating half-brother to half-sister to protect the purity of the blood-line, that many malformations, including deafness and other congenital disorders, had begun to manifest themselves. Strains of bulldog bred to the famous Paddington White, a noted bulldog of 1819, were later to become extinct as a consequence of congenital disorders of this nature. Even so, Major Malcolm of Poltalloch kept white puppies from Cairn litters and produced his pack of West Highland white terriers which were in no way short in courage or constitution if the stories concerning the pack's exploits on Skye and in the Highlands were true. It is nevertheless reasonable to assume that white-bodied working terriers were rare in the British country-side prior to 1800.

How, therefore, did the white-bodied working terrier appear – or, more to the point, why did such a coloration materialize? The most commonly held theory, repeated *ad nauseam* in almost every Jack Russell terrier book, is that, during the 1700s, fox hunting, using properly organized packs of hounds, became popular. To bolt the foxes and allow the hounds a run, a terrier therefore had to be used. These books argue that a white-bodied working terrier was fairly essential for such a task, since hounds might mistake a brown or black-and-tan terrier for a fox and kill the terrier. Certainly this is something which happens from time to time, though it is fair to mention that hounds which chop brown terriers will chop white ones equally readily. It should also be mentioned that the Northern hunts, who have always used Border and Lakeland terriers and other coloured terriers, rarely have such mishaps, and such tragedies are far more common in the hunting shires than in the Fells. The theory that white-bodied working terriers came into being merely to bolt foxes for hound packs does not therefore entirely stand up to close examination, and my own theory as to why they appeared is a little more complex.

During the eighteenth century, two events were to alter the British terrier far more than the arrival of properly organized fox hunting. It was during this period and into the early nineteenth century that the ignominious sport of badger baiting or badger drawing was enjoy-ing its final fling. Even in 1800, public opinion was turning decidedly against this sort of sport, and Kellow Chesney, in his *The Victorian Underworld*, hints that only the lowest classes of society enjoyed such spectacles. Badger drawing was, in fact, a curious sort of spectacle, as inane as it was cruel. It consisted of tethering a badger inside a barrel and encouraging a terrier to rush in and drag the luckless beast from its fastness, whereupon some idiot would bite the dog's tail to make it release the badger. Prizes were awarded – and pitiful and pathetic prizes they were, sometimes no more than a bottle of lemonade – for the dog who could draw out the badger the greatest number of times in a said period; or, quite simply, for the dog who could pull out the badger the greatest number of times without quitting cold. Inane as it was, there are tales of amazing chicanery told of the sport. One tale quoted by Fitzbarnard in his *Fighting Sports*, is of a character who won amazing sums by betting that his dog would draw a particular badger an incredible number of times in a said period. When some worthies visited the owner of the dog, they found the terrier asleep in its kennel, the other occupant of which was its friend the badger.

One thing was certain, that when the event was staged properly (if 'properly' could ever be an appropriate word) the sport required a most courageous and hard terrier to tackle a badger the number of times which some of these dogs did, and the native British terrier was simply not tough enough. The sport was officially abolished in 1835, along with such other nauseating spectacles as bull baiting and dog fighting, but during the first half of the nineteenth century the sport enjoyed a great upsurge in interest, as Alkens's prints of 1820 seem to indicate. If the native British terrier was not hard enough, a type of dog which was lay close at hand, for the British bulldog was the most valiant beast the Almighty (assisted by a number of sadistic breeders) had chosen to create.

Yet another trend destined to alter the appearance and structure of the British working terrier was the popularizing of the sport of competitive rat killing, for the brown rat, which appeared in our islands in 1720, give or take a few years, had established itself in such numbers as to become not only a major health hazard, but also the staple sporting quarry of the working classes. Henry Mayhew actually describes the sport of competitive rat slaughter as 'the last remaining poor man's sport'. For the arena, a pit was made – usually between six and ten feet square of either netting or boards – and a dozen or so rats were tipped into the enclosure, where they milled about and pitifully awaited an ugly death. They did not have long to wait, for as a bell was sounded a terrier would be placed in the pit. The dog who killed the greatest number of rats in the shortest period was deemed to be the winner.

The nineteenth century was certainly an amazing period in history, when the British public delighted in killing, maiming and crippling against the clock. Most terriers would quickly see off a dozen or so rats, but, for the bigger league stuff, where sums of money were wagered on dogs killing a hundred or a thousand rats, a very game dog was required and a constitutionally sound dog at that, for timed carnage of this nature requires a prodigiously fit and game beast. The native British terrier was simply not up to such work – it was neither bred nor designed for coping with such quantities of these immigrant creatures. So, once again, man resorted to using the native British bulldog to cross with the British terriers to produce a dog suitable for the rat-pit contests.

Let the reader at once dismiss the notion that these bulldogs were the same monstrosities that we see today, puffing and panting after any minor exertion. The real bulldog, the bulldog of the 1800s, was a devil incarnate. He had been bred for baiting bulls, for holding the bull by the nostrils or face and holding with such tenacity that his grip became a legend, as did his courage. He was also fought against other dogs, monkeys and men, and even once or twice against a lion, and his courage and tenacity did much to delight the rabble who relished such feasts of gore. As to his courage, well, no one could question it, it was bottomless. All he lacked were the nimble qualities, the agility that a good badger-baiting dog and rat-pit virtuoso required. Hence a judicious blend of terrier and bulldog, having the terrier's speed and agility and the incredible guts of the bulldog, provided the ideal dog.

These bull and terriers were a mixed lot, ranging in size from 60-pound Blue Pauls, popular in Scotland and the North of England, to 9-pound to 12-pound grapplers, like the now extinct Cheshire terrier, a breed used by John Tucker Edwardes to boost the courage of his Sealyham terriers. Now most of the noted strains of pit bulldog were either pied or white, and so, by dint of crossing these terriers with these bulldogs, white earth dogs began to appear – white dogs that left even the diehards of the North in no doubt as to their courage and constitution, for several of these strains were introduced into the base stock which produced the Bedlington and the Dandie Dinmont terriers.

In this way the native terrier underwent a change, and the newly emergent white-bodied working terrier was to be the ancestor of the Jack Russell terrier of today. To be honest, it was also to be the ancestor of the more elegant fox terrier, for there is little evidence to suggest that the fox terrier was a cross between the old English white terrier and the broken-coated black and tan terrier, as most dog books seem to imply, and while John Russell was said to have detested the bull-blooded terriers for crushing the 'gentlemanly character' of the breed, he was almost alone in this belief. Ash, a contemporary of the parson, mentions that it was 'all the rage' to produce plucky terriers by hybridizing terrier types with bulldogs; and Sparrow, as late as 1930, advocated bringing in bull terrier blood every ten or so generations to keep up courage and size of jaw in working terriers. In fact it may be said that, with the exception of the Scottish breeds, few breeds of British terrier do not owe their courage and constitution to a liberal dash of bulldog blood. Such utter fearlessness, such blind courage, does, however, have its drawbacks.

The bulldog, and, indeed, the bulldog hybrid, is an aggressive beast which tends to close with its prey rather than baying at it and encouraging it to bolt. Furthermore, the bulldog type of dog fights by simply taking a hold and keeping its grip until a more lethal holding point can be attained. Thus they fight silently, with only a grunt or a roar to indicate their presence. Such a terrier is practically useless if worked with hounds; at least, it is in the South, where terriers are required to bolt a fox rather than slay it below ground as many northern terriers are bred to do. Furthermore, a dog which fights its fox silently is damn nigh impossible to dig to. And while the bull-blooded dog may do well against fox, when he meets a badger things are likely to be somewhat different and the dog who tackles a fully grown badger will discover to his cost the mistake he has made. Thus a bull-blooded dog with a fair percentage of bulldog blood has its limitations as a terrier.

This is why another ingredient was sometimes added to the potent mix of bulldog and terrier: namely, the beagle. The Earl of March, in his *Records of the Old Charlton Hunt*, mentions a poem advocating the mating of beagles with very hard terriers to produce a dog with both nose sense and voice; and since beagles are predominantly white-bodied, the white-bodied working terrier was not greatly altered by this cross, except that the progeny were decidedly more useful as hunt terriers. It was from this morass or mixture that the modern Jack Russell arose together with the fox terrier (many of which have hound markings so similar to those of the beagle that hound ancestry is obvious). That was how the mongrelly, so-called Jack Russell terrier remained until well into the twentieth century, and the first hunt terrier shows I attended in the 1950s were indeed extraordinary sights, with the most amazingly variable types of dog being proudly shown as genuine Jack Russells; some of them displayed hints of collie, or, not infrequently, dachshund, in their lineage. Many were quite hideous, but handsome is as handsome does, and some of those monstrosities proved to be incredibly good workers.

During the 1960s, however, hunt shows became increasingly

Worker and champion: Greg Mouseley's Rastus. A supreme champion and holder of an MFH Working Certificate.

Eddie Chapman's Sinbad – an under 11" champion and holder of an MFH Working Certificate.

popular, far more popular than they are today, and gradually the seeds of a future standard were sown. Certain judges even tried to implement the supposed yardstick of John Russell, but there was little genuine uniformity to judging in those days. Gradually, however, the ugly little dogs who made up the majority of hunt terrier classes began to alter, sometimes by judicious breeding from sires of good types, but more frequently quite simply by crossing with other breeds which had the characteristics desired by show judges: namely, straight fronts and narrow chests, reach of neck and so on. Several excellent Russell types of terrier were bred by quite simply introducing the blood of Border and Lakeland terriers, and these were not a whit the worse for their mixed origins. In the North, fox terriers were mated to the Russell types of terrier, and although finer, neater, straight-legged dogs were bred, with this finer bone there came weaker jaws. Yet breeders like Derek Hume managed to produce excellent stock – excellent both in the hunting field and at shows. Other breeds were used to ameliorate the hunt terrier. Brockley's famous bitch, Tussle, showed obvious beagle influence, while one of the most famous 10-inch rough-coated studs of the late 1960s was bred from mating two half-bred Norfolk x Jack Russell terriers and keeping the white-bodied puppies. I took several bitches to this dog and produced some very neat, game little terriers who not only won well in shows, but also did well as ratting terriers and worked fox and badger along with the best. One famous northern Jack Russell, a 14-inch dog – a little tall and spare for my liking – was actually a sport or genetic throwback bred from two very lean and rangy black Fell terriers who quite obviously had Bedlington terrier not too far back in their ancestry.

Today such crossings, even judicious blendings, are frowned upon, but most of the really classy Jack Russells shown today owe at least some of their looks to Kennel Club registered breeds being infused into the stock during the 1960s, and this frankly did little to harm the breed at all. I must confess that my famous stud dog, Warlock – a noted producer of his day – is a blend of beagle, pit bull terrier, fox terrier and Jack Russell, and is certainly under no disadvantage with his mixed ancestry. Even so, the policy of the recently formed Jack Russell Club of Great Britain is to frown on such crosses, and it is to the club itself that we will now turn our attention.

2 THE JACK RUSSELL CLUB OF GREAT BRITAIN

Before considering the history and aims of the Jack Russell Club of Great Britain, it is essential to say at least a few words about its founder, Mrs Romayne Moore, for few people have done as much to promote the Jack Russell terrier as has this lady. Prior to the formation of the present group, Mrs Moore founded another working terrier club, the Midland Working Terrier Club, which was a society concerned with various breeds of working terrier. This club did much to publicize the working terrier, and besides the shows it ran also produced a useful magazine which contained numerous excellent articles concerned with all aspects of terrier work. In fact, some of the best advice concerning working terriers I have ever read was contained within the pages of that periodical. Late in the 1960s, Mrs Moore left Britain for Uganda, and like the Macedonian Empire on the death of Alexander, the club literally fell to pieces. It continued with flagging membership well into the 1970s, but before the formation of the Jack Russell Club of Great Britain, the Midland Working Terrier Club had become nearly extinct, partly because of lack of enthusiasm among its members, but primarily because of some competition from the Fell and Moorland Working Terrier Club – a well-organized association that not only produced a better type of magazine, but also offered a rescue service for any terrier which became trapped below ground.

On her return from Uganda, Mrs Moore was somewhat saddened to find that the club she had formed had collapsed and promptly set about forming a club for Jack Russell terrier owners. Early in 1975, she sent out questionnaires asking various terrier breeders about the standard of excellence that might be drawn up for the Jack Russell terrier. The replies she received were nothing short of extraordinary, ranging from descriptions which might have been culled from Davies's biography of John Russell to descriptions which seemed more to match a white-bodied dachshund. Then, in 1975, a show was staged in Stoneleigh, Warwickshire, and after a rather heated meeting, a number of people were elected to form a committee for the purpose of founding the Jack Russell Terrier Club of Great Britain.

This embryonic committee met later that year to elect officers, and, regretfully, I was elected to the position of chairman. I am forced to say regretfully, for not only had I no experience of the duties of a chairman, but I am temperamentally a little like Kipling's cat and prefer to walk alone. Furthermore, it is said that people become very like their dogs, and the members of the newly formed club provided some support for this particular theory. Conditions of near-riot prevailed at meetings during the early days of the club, partly arising from the aggression of various members of the committee and partly because of my own inadequacy as chairman. Thankfully, I was supported by Mrs Moore and her husband throughout my term of office. During the first meeting, a standard of sorts was drawn up, based almost exactly on the standard outlined in my earlier book, *The Jack Russell Terrier, Its Training and Entering*. With a few pieces of tidying up, that standard is still used by the club. (See the Appendix, page 157.) For some reason which I have never really been able to understand, brindle markings on a terrier were to be regarded as undesirable by the standard to be adopted.

Several other fiery meetings followed the first, and the Advance Register was formed. Briefly, any dog that conformed to a rough description of a Jack Russell terrier was eligible for registration in the initial register, but only certain dogs above eighteen months old, of a supposed high standard of excellence, legs, fronts, type and so forth, were to be allowed to be entered in the Advanced Register, and these had to be passed as suitable for the register by specially appointed inspectors. While, as chairman, I had no vote in the passing of this motion, I spoke against the register as unnecessary, since I did not see such a register as likely to be helpful in the improvement of the Jack Russell terrier, which was the reason for forming the register. A far better way of creating a more homogeneous group would have been to follow the advice of Haagedoorn, the leading (if now somewhat discredited) Dutch geneticist who advocated that, if the noted winners in dog shows were well advertised, many would use them in preference to inferior dogs; and thus, with a limitation of the number of sires used, the breed would become more homogeneous. As it turned out, some of the inspectors were too strict and failed a majority of dogs, while others were far too lenient and passed most terriers, even those with bent legs, bad mouths and other physical malformations. So bad were some of the specimens passed for the Advanced Register that, at the 1978 Welsh Section Show, a guffaw of laughter emerged from the crowd when the Advanced Register class was called. Frankly, the specimens were exceedingly bad. Still, just as the terrier itself will become more

Rona Marvin's Meg, an excellent under 11" rough. Good small, rough-coated terriers are very difficult to breed.

uniform, so will the standards of the Advanced Register inspectors – at least, so it is to be hoped.

At the moment of writing, a group of some thirty members, headed by Mrs Roma Moore, is urging the Kennel Club to accept the Jack Russell terrier into its folds. Many in the club are, however, opposed to this move, since it is believed that Kennel Club recognition could ruin the working qualities of the breed. This assumption is a little ludicrous if one examines it closely with a modicum of thought and common sense (sadly rare commodities in dog breeders, I'm afraid), for the Kennel Club has little or no influence over whether members work their terriers or, indeed, strive to keep the working qualities of the breed alive. It remains the duty of breeders and exhibitors to ensure that the dog is kept as a working breed. Furthermore, various splinter groups of the Jack Russell Terrier Club of Great Britain have recently been formed, each with its own rules and standards. Recognition of the breed by the Central Committee of the Kennel Club would at least allow a peaceful, orderly and organized coalescence of these clubs, and would improve at least some rules of the standards of behaviour of members at shows and committee meetings.

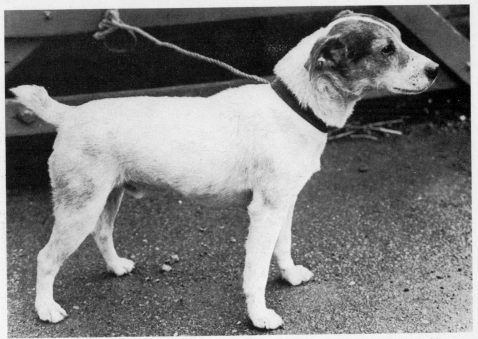

Alan Thomas' Hamish, an over 11" champion and holder of an MFH Working Certificate.

For those whose interest in the breed is exhibition rather than work (and not everyone wishes to work or has facilities to work his terriers), Kennel Club recognition allows at least some redress of grievance for some of the ridiculous judging decisions that are all too common at the splinter groups' club shows. Should the Kennel Club decide to allow the Jack Russell terrier into its fold, it will be the duty of the breeders of these dogs to determine the fate of these terriers.

3 CHOOSING A TERRIER

Perhaps it is the best piece of advice contained in this book to say that, if one is going to purchase a terrier, then buy a puppy and avoid the purchase of an adult terrier at all costs. There are very few Jack Russell terrier breeders in Britain who are not plagued by inquiries for trained and entered terriers – inquiries which, I must add, fill me with disgust. Such people are usually enjoying a brief spell as hunters, and next year will have tired of their trained terrier, passed it on to another, or traded it for bantams, pigeons or such like. They are also, by inquiring after a trained terrier, mutely admitting to the fact that they are unable to train a terrier for themselves, though most blandly disguise this by the statement, 'I haven't time to train one myself.' It is an admission of failure to purchase a trained terrier.

Dealers in trained, or partly trained (a tongue-in-cheek expression, for partly trained dogs are never sold) terriers abound, and their kennels are usually transit camps for rejected and dejected dogs: dogs who have suffered psychologically by repeated changes of home, dogs that have failed their hasty owners, and dogs that are passing along a chain of ephemeral hunters, destined for what is euphemistically known as an animal shelter, or canine knackers yard, where many will undoubtedly finish their days. Personally, I find dog dealing just a little distasteful, since most dealers in adult dogs simply contribute to the confusion and misery experienced by a terrier which is passed from kennel to kennel. Perhaps such change of ownership does little harm to the greyhound type of dog, as the amazing trade in lurchers probably testifies, but to a dog with the temperament and psychological make-up of a terrier, the effect can only be devastating. Even so, dealers are essential, if only to act as a somewhat temporary sanctuary for dogs who are in the process of being passed on by dissatisfied, unsuccessful terrier trainers.

Reader, consider the purchase of a trained terrier logically before dipping your hand into your pocket to make a purchase of a grown dog, and do not senselessly hurl your money down the drain by making a hasty purchase. It takes roughly two years to train a terrier properly, and sometimes even longer to take it through the spectrum of quarry from rat to fox to badger. Two years of hard graft are needed to make (or, whisper it, to break) a dog into a properly trained terrier that is free from the vices of viciousness and stock worrying,

24

obedient and reliable. Few people will sell you such a dog, a dog that will have been their very reason for existence over the last two years, for, make no bones about it, the training of a terrier is an all-consuming task. There probably do exist men who are forced into selling their terriers by force of circumstance, and stories of men whose marriages have broken up (a fairly common occurrence when terrier work is a man's *raison d'être*, the reader should be warned) are legion. But, again, it should be emphasized that most true terrier men will endure great hardship rather than sell their wards. I once lived in a large shed with my terriers rather than sell them, but then I find the word 'eccentric' less offensive than the term 'dog dealer'. Hence the possibility of purchasing a good, reliable, honest working dog, trained with expertise by a terrier man, becomes extremely remote. Sufficient to say I would never consider buying a trained terrier, or a trained dog of any breed, for that matter.

Saplings – dogs just out of puppyhood, but not old enough to be classed as adults – are often offered for sale, and provided these have not been ruined by premature entering, they might be regarded as a fair purchase. Many have been 'run on' by show breeders and have not become the winners their owners hoped they might turn out to be, and so are more often than not offered for sale at a ridiculously low price to ensure the dog receives a good home. These, however, will more than likely have missed the preliminary training a hunting dog should receive, and many will have developed vices during their time with their owner/breeder. Moreover, few terriers intended for a life on the show bench will have had the preliminary encouragement that a hunter would have given his puppy, and so these saplings may take far longer to enter to quarry than might be expected.

For the beginner who wishes to work Jack Russell terriers, it would be extremely sensible to purchase a puppy at the outset, not that you are out of the woods with the purchase of a six- or eight-week-old babe. Choose your purchase with care. Always ask to see the parents of the pups – the dam will nearly always be available, and it would be good advice to seek out and examine the size of the pups one is considering buying. If the sire and dam are not what you consider to be your ideal Jack Russell terrier, nor approximate to it, do not purchase. Take time before parting with your money, view other litters, examine other sires and dams before making your purchase. It is wise to remember that, at the time of writing, the Kennel Club has not opened its doors to the motley collection of dogs collectively and conveniently known as Jack Russell terriers, so frankly any white-bodied puppy can be sold as a Jack Russell terrier without fear of violation of the Trades Descriptions Act.

25

My mother's favourite saying was 'Marry in haste, repent at leisure,' and the same should be said of the purchase of a terrier. A story will illustrate the point. Twelve years ago, a close friend came to get a puppy as a birthday present for his young daughter. I had no puppies at the time, so he had collected a whole pile of advertisements from local newspapers and requested that I should go and help him to choose one. Frankly, this is a task I dislike, for not only is one usually held responsible for an unsatisfactory or unhealthy purchase, but traffic between kennels is a great spreader of disease. I've had distemper brought to my kennels through curious sightseers, bands of whom haunt various kennels as a Sunday afternoon day out. Against my better judgement, we went to see a litter, the advertisement for which had read, 'Farm-reared Jack Russell Terriers.' We arrived at the smallholding and were greeted by a rather attractive though portly Jack Russell bitch which was obviously suckling a litter. So far so good. Now to view the puppies. They were a remarkably even lot – that is, if one likes black and white collie-marked puppies. I asked to see the sire, and was told by the wife that it belonged to her brother who lived in Thetford – a matter of two hundred miles away, and sufficiently far to prevent us from visiting him, I thought. I touched my friend's arm as an indication we should leave without the purchase of a puppy, for anyone who will travel two hundred miles to mate a bitch when there are superb stud dogs available locally is a bit suspect. But he seemed adamant that he was going to buy one in spite of my warnings. We left, and the farmer waved us good-bye, accompanied by his collie dog, which oddly enough had markings that exactly resembled my friend's new terrier puppy. Twelve years later, my friend's daughter married and moved with her now elderly dog to a new house three miles from home. Oddly, it closely resembles a dark-tailed collie – a much-loved pet, of course, but hardly a Jack Russell terrier.

But let us assume you have found your would-be purchase and are delighted with the look of the parents – that is, of course, if they are the parents, and not simply a pair of glamorous starlets hired for your visit. What comes next? Well, yet another lesson needs to be learnt, this time in psychology, before you part with your hard-earned cash. Talk to the owner of the puppies. If he comes out with the 'I'm a hard man who likes a hard dog' stuff, then *caveat emptor*, let the buyer beware indeed. Hard in terrier parlance is usually equated with ignorance or indifference, so the chances are that your would-be purchase has been reared without heat and fed on the poorest quality food – treatment which, contrary to creating a tough little beast, produces a puppy that will give you a fair deal of trouble in his later life. Then watch the dam of the pups. Few well-fed bitches with puppies that are eight weeks old will be 'down' or in bad condition – that is, if they and their whelps have been fed properly. If she has not been fed properly, she will look haggard, very thin, even emaciated and exhausted; and if she has been badly fed, her pups will not have been fed properly either.

Similarly, avoid the pups of a bitch that is displaying bare or bald patches, despite the owner's bland standard reassurance, 'Oh, yes she always has a patch or so of eczema whenever she whelps'. As a rule it will not be eczema, which is not infectious. It is far more likely to be one of the two unpleasant types of mange which is causing this redness – and some mange, unlike eczema, is highly contagious and invariably shows itself at such times of stress as after a bad mauling from a fox or badger, or after an illness or teething, or, let it be again whispered, after whelping. Should you disregard my advice and purchase your puppy, then the odds will be 100:1 that at not more than five months of age, your puppy will need a great deal of expensive veterinary treatment to combat the mange that has mysteriously manifested itself the moment he started to get his permanent teeth. How very odd.

Another point to remember as your child is cuddling her newly purchased puppy on the homeward trip is that mange is also known as scabies – of which more later in the book – but your child won't need to wait very long before an unpleasant, irritating and embarrassing skin disease begins to manifest itself. But then, there's just another novelty that may be acquired free of charge with a hasty purchase.

So far so good, but what are the other hazards? Examine your aspiring purchase closely. Don't buy a pot-bellied puppy who is obviously wormy. Very well, so you *can* worm him, but bear in mind, first, that your puppy will have his condition reduced by the shock of changing homes, so the additional shock of worming him won't exactly help his constitution; secondly, that any breeder worth his salt will have wormed his pups prior to selling them; and thirdly, that worms can and will infect young children in your household, causing not merely gastric disorders, but possibly also an extremely unpleasant complaint known as viceral larval migrans – a disease which can lead to blindness in a child. Therefore ask the owner if he has wormed them, and ask to see the chemical he has used as a vermifuge. If it is a proprietary roundworm remedy, all well and good, but if it is one of the hoary oldies, like a cud of chewing tobacco rammed down the babe's throat or, horror of horrors, a ground glass and castor oil mix, then bid the vendor a quiet and respectful good-bye and get the hell out of his madhouse. Such worming mixes belong in the world of witchcraft rather than of science, though the reader would be surprised how often they are still used. Sufficient to say that such mixtures don't exactly help the puppy. If you are damned fool enough to buy a puppy from a tinker site, or one from freshly settled gipsies, you may well find that such worming mediums are all too commonly used to this day. So much for the 'natural methods' sometimes eulogized by writers who know little of the ways of itinerants.

Again, avoid the thin-furred and lean puppy. 'Aye, I allus likes a pup a bit lean,' the vendor will tell you. Babes should be fat and round. The thin-furred, emaciated beast has either been (a) badly reared; or (b) previously or currently sick; or (c) reared in cold conditions. The cause of its poor condition shouldn't worry you. Reach for your coat and say good-bye. This is not the puppy for you, regardless of the insistence of the vendor and the bleat of your child who, like all children, usually grows most enthusiastic about any sick and ailing creature. You may have tears at your failure to purchase, but they will be as nothing compared to the tears when you come to bury the puppy.

But now we may assume that you have convinced yourself as to the reliability of your breeder, have noted that his bitch and her puppies are in good fettle, have realized that he is breeding exactly what you are after. The time has come to choose the puppy. *Go for the boldest in the litter.* Choose the one who is scrambling out of the box to greet you, wetting himself in excitement at the thought of someone new to play with – the real extrovert, the genuine 100 per cent sycophant. Avoid the one which shyly stays out of range, coyly aloof and nervous, who holds his tail down as he avoids your gaze. Disregard wife and kids as they say how they fancy a quiet one, a puppy who is appealing, who is not boisterous. That is not the puppy for you. Terriers, Jack Russells at least (Borders are a bit different, I admit) are by nature brash and extrovert, and the shy one will usually reward your purchase of him by skulking under furniture as a puppy and biting savagely when older. Few bold terriers bite, but the shy, nervous biters can be very, very dangerous indeed. A shy, nervous terrier is a liability to end all liabilities when it grows older, for cringing, frightened dogs always act like a magnet to children, and the results are often catastrophic. I should also be very, very cagey about buying a puppy whose parents were touchy with people, for such traits, though sometimes simply acquired through bad or foolish treatment, are as often as not inherited.

The time has come to correct two fallacies. The reader, let us assume, has had his eye caught by an advertisement for Jack Russells, the appraisal for which reads 'From good working stock.' First fallacy about to explode: such puppies will *not* grow into mean little psychopaths, ever eager to savage livestock and children alike, even if they are bought as pets. Working Russells are usually very even tempered, for the cause of most of the biting which one hears about is simply nervousness, not courage. Nervous dogs are of little use to the hunter; I never put them up in shows and avoid taking them on if I can. Pups from working dogs will usually be good prospects, even as pets.

Next fallacy about to explode: the advertisement reads 'From such and such a hunt strain.' Do not imagine you will get anything special from this blood, for few hunts have strains and the dogs usually go with the terrier man when he changes hunts. Furthermore, a great number of hunt terriers are simply gift dogs given to the terrier man by hunt supporters and such like as adults for various reasons – savage or perhaps over-energetic dogs frequently find their way to hunts. Maybe before the Second World War or earlier, some hunts did have their own strains of terrier. John Cobby certainly did, as did Capel, but today most hunts keep an odd assortment of terriers at their kennels. To get an idea, the reader should visit the local hunt – and will find that in fact any type of dog which will go to ground and do the job may be seen at the majority of hunt kennels. Thus an advertisement for such and such a hunt's strain of terrier may provide a puppy that proves satisfactory, but they will be no more blue-blooded than the dogs available from a breeder on your near-by council estate. The same applies to 'as worked by game-keeper' recommendations, I might also add. These terriers are nothing special just because a gamekeeper owns them.

Treat 'farm reared' with a bit of reservation as well. I've seen some hellish conditions in farm kennels, and as the farm is usually outside the Public Health Acts, literally appalling conditions can escape prosecution. I have seen on one farm in Wales, a farm which purports to specialize in Border collies and Jack Russells, kennelling that merits the owner receiving a horse whipping rather than prosecution. A litter which I saw reared at this hell hole, as yet unnoticed by our amazingly lax and lethargic public health officials, was whelped under a filthy, leaky, poultry shed in an excavated rat warren. Two of the puppies survived, and no doubt their purchasers proudly boasted that their dogs were 'farm reared'. Not all farmers treat their puppies in this manner, of course, but the term 'farm reared' does not always mean that the babes have been reared in a land of milk and honey. Examine the premises where the puppies were reared before you part with your money.

So, you've eventually made your choice, having run the gauntlet of the advice just ladled out. You have purchased your puppy – aged eight weeks or more – have decided that he is what you want, and it's home you go with your purchase. The very best of luck to you – the purchase is just the beginning of the long endurance course that will, if all goes well, culminate in the rearing and training of the dog and its eventual entering to quarry. But that lies some time distant. First rear your puppy; the entering comes later, and, if you have any sense, much later, for premature entering has been the ruination of many a good terrier.

4 REARING A PUPPY

We have therefore reached the point where the puppy has left the vendor and arrived at the home of the buyer. First piece of advice: don't expect to sleep well the first night after purchasing a young puppy. Your purchase will have been accustomed to the warmth and security of its dam and the company of its litter brothers and sisters. He has now been rudely and abruptly snatched away from a familiar environment and placed in a somewhat alien world. As soon as the puppy arrives home, he will gladly welcome his new-found extra attention, and during the evening will appear to be quite pleased with his lot. But, as soon as darkness falls and the family retires to bed, the whelp begins to understand the meaning of loneliness for the first time in its brief life, and reacts accordingly, usually by howling in the most plaintive manner.

It is hard for anyone to resist such pathetic cries, and at this point many families take the puppy to bed with them – where it continues to spend every night of its life until senility. Therefore resist the urge to rush down and comfort the puppy, or to take it into bed. The howling may be reduced by placing a hot-water bottle in the pup's box or basket, or by standing a loud-ticking alarm clock in the same room as the puppy. It usually works simply because the ticking breaks the monotony of the night and gives the puppy some interest. It has nothing to do with imitating the heart beat of the dam – an opinion so often expressed in many dog books.

Diet is the next problem. Puppies need to eat little and often: as much as they will eat, four times a day. Irish greyhound breeders often leave quantities of meat for the saplings, and the running dogs of Ireland are legendary. This method is, however, thwart with danger. Food left down the whole day becomes uninteresting and begins to decompose. The puppy who is forced to eat it will suffer from acute gastric disorders. Feed regularly, and four times a day is not too often, and throw away any food not eaten at once – never put it aside for later.

The staple food of a puppy should be flesh, but the new purchase should be kept on the same diet as the breeder has been feeding him for several days and new foods introduced only gradually. The whole art of puppy rearing is, quite simply, to prevent the puppy from experiencing gastric disorders. Diarrhoea is fairly normal the first day or two after purchase, but, should it persist, take the whelp straight to the vet. Home-made remedies for diarrhoea, such as dry toast or arrowroot, will only work if the cause is not bacterial. Persistent diarrhoea is probably the greatest killer of newly purchased puppies, for such puppies lose body water rapidly, and the results of dehydration are often pitiful to see. *Persistent diarrhoea needs expert professional attention.*

Meat should make up the greatest part of the diet. It can be provided in the form of canned meat or butcher's waste or offal. Avoid feeding lights or spleen (called melt by butchers), since these are not very nourishing and also have a laxative effect. Tripe or paunch is a useful stand-by. I am not happy about feeding large quantities of cereal to puppies, nor about feeding complete foods with a high cereal content. Such foods usually produce puppies with rather fleshless rib cages, and they do not usually thrive on a low meat diet. Some years ago, my local vet had merry hell convincing a very cranky and determined vegetarian woman that the cause of ill health in her Pekinese puppy was the absence of meat in his diet. If you are an ardent vegetarian, or, worse still, a vegan, who will touch no animal produce and has strong moral beliefs about meat, don't own a dog. Your recently acquired beliefs will certainly clash with your animal's digestive tracts, which have altered very little since his domestication over a million years ago. Dogs need flesh. Dried meat is a useful and cheap stand-by for adult dogs once they are accustomed to the food, but will be damned nigh fatal to a newly purchased puppy unless he has been fed on such a diet before you purchased him. Dried meat has a violent emetic effect on a puppy's dietary tract, and can render it down to a dehydrated skeleton before it becomes accustomed to the food.

Now for a seemingly pointless piece of information. During the golden age of the public schools, just after Arnold was head of Rugby, it was common practice to place the heads of infant bed wetters down the newly invented flushing lavatories and pull the chain. Clearly this was an inane and pointless action, as any reasonably normal reader must realize. Yet it is surprising how many people will endeavour to house-train a puppy by rubbing its nose in its excreta or urine. Frankly, the act is just as ludicrous as trying to cure bed wetting by holding people's heads down a toilet. House-training is easy if one can be with a puppy all day long. It should take maybe two weeks to house-train a dog under these circumstances – though considerably longer if one has to be out for a large part of the day. House-training is simply the creating of acceptable habits, and if the puppy's toilet habits are observed carefully for a day or so, it will be extremely easy to house-train him. First, a puppy usually urinates a matter of moments after waking up, and almost immediately after eating. Thus a puppy who has just awoken or eaten should immediately be put out of doors, where it will get into the habit of fouling and wetting well clear of the house.

Fallacy-exploding time again, I fear. It is a common belief that a hunting dog should never be allowed the attention of children and be kept in splendid isolation from the family, any contact with children reputedly making a dog soft. This is, in fact, a huge, howling fallacy – and not only is it illogical, but it goes against the scientific fact that a puppy reared in isolation, away from children, human company, noise and bustle, suffers quite badly mentally and becomes less tractable than a socialized puppy. Some years ago, a psychologist named Hebb had some beagle puppies reared in isolation, a similar batch of puppies being farmed out among his fellow psychologists and reared in houses where they had contact with young children. At the age of six months, both batches were taken up for training; and the puppies reared in isolation proved nervous, stupid and intractable, whereas the other batch of socialized puppies proved easy to train – or at least easy to train for beagles, who are not among the canine geniuses. Of course, this fact had been known to fox hunters for centuries before Hebb was born, and it has long been the practice for hunts to farm out puppies to grow up in contact with families, thereby allowing them to become more responsive to training.

Until a puppy is inoculated, he should not venture out of doors. Unlike Germany, where it is illegal to allow dogs to roam the streets, Britain has, at the time of writing, hosts of wandering dogs in its towns – dogs which urinate on and foul the pavements, leaving trees, telegraph poles and lamp-posts alive with myriad infections that can cause serious illnesses in an uninoculated puppy. One survey taken in Glasgow revealed that very few marking points – that is, places where dogs urinate – were not literally havens for the deadly hepatitis virus.

Shortly after a puppy is born, his dam secretes colestrum, a yellow first milk which is rich in protective antibodies that give a degree of limited protection against most of the deadly infections that dogs are heir to. (Some antibodies are also passed across the placenta – a fact often unknown even by some vets.) By the time the puppy is twelve weeks old, most of the antibodies will have been destroyed in the puppy's body, leaving the whelp open to infection. It is therefore absolutely necessary to inoculate a dog against the four deadly evils: distemper, hard pad, hepatitis and leptospirosis, each one as destructive as an apocalyptic horseman.

Immunization usually consists of two injections, the first being an

33

Terriers should be absolutely 'steady' with livestock.

injection of weakened distemper and hepatitis virus together with a dose of leptospirosis inoculant, and the second, some two weeks later, of leptospirosis, which boosts the effect of the first inoculation. Disregard those who advise that such inoculations are not only unnecessary but also totally worthless. Such immunization is absolutely essential for the pet, and particularly for any hunting dog. Sufficient to say that no reputable boarding kennels will take in an uninoculated dog, and while it cannot be claimed that inoculation is 100 per cent effective, during the 1968 distemper outbreak, when literally hundreds of uninoculated dogs died, I did not lose an inoculated dog, nor do I know of anyone who did. Inoculation is quite simply essential for the working terrier.

Another pair of essentials are lead training and stock breaking. Both should be taught quite young. Lead training can be done indoors, even prior to inoculation, and is so remarkably easy that it is unnecessary to relate how it should be carried out. Puppies should also be introduced to stock as soon as they are inoculated. Take the puppy among sheep and cattle; allow calves, the most curious of beasts, to rush up to him and terrify him. It may on the face of it seem a little harsh, but puppies who experience fear of stock at this age rarely develop into stock worriers. My own puppies are taken ratting at fourteen weeks old, not with the notion of getting them to kill rats, but because this is the ideal age for them to be broken to poultry, and most of my ratting is done in battery houses.

This is also the time for puppies to realize that ferrets are not fair game, but simply helpmates in the hunt. Allow ferrets to run among the puppies, to sniff and even nip them; and chastize any puppy who tries to attack a ferret. A ferret nipped by a puppy suffers little harm, but a ferret bitten by an adult terrier rarely survives the attack. It is imperative to have working terriers broken to ferret, for such terriers can then easily be entered to rats which are bolted by ferrets. Furthermore, in a country that is rapidly becoming a huge metropolis where every form of hunting territory is growing scarce, a terrier broken to ferret can provide endless sport in ratting, for the most unpleasant places in urban districts harbour myriads of rats. Frankly, I loathe using anyone else's terriers when I am ratting, since it's dollars to doughnuts that I will finish up the day with a dead ferret. And having stock-worrying terriers is not only a nuisance, it also proves that the terrier's owner is a crass amateur. Furthermore, in a country where it is difficult to get any form of hunting, a man with a stock-worrying terrier will be most unlikely to receive a welcome anywhere.

By the time a puppy is five months old, the owner will have noticed numerous changes, both physiological and psychological. The pup will have shed most of his deciduous milk teeth and have developed a far more adult approach to life. Furthermore, fights among puppies of this age are usually extremely furious and ferocious affairs, triggered off by seemingly pointless situations. Such behaviour is common in all canines of this age, and in the case of jackals and wolves it results in the formation of some form of social hierarchy, some sort of law of peck. In the case of foxes, it leads to the breaking up and dispersal of the litter. In the case of the working terrier, such an upsurge in aggression should be taken as an indication that the terrier is nearly ready to enter to quarry – which brings us to the next section of the book.

5 ENTERING THE PUPPY TO QUARRY

The Rat

For reasons dealt with in great detail in my book *The Working Terrier* (1978), it is wise to start young puppies on rats and to progress through stoats and similar quarry to fox and ultimately badger. I have to confess that my best sport has been obtained in hunting rats. Little else can match it for sheer speed, excitement and entertainment. Furthermore, few beasts are more loathsome than rats, so the hunter feels little qualm about killing them. Also, in spite of modern hygiene, and almost absurd public health restrictions, it is one of the few animals actually on the increase in our overcrowded island, largely because the government has, in its questionable wisdom, placed farms outside public health inspection regulations.

Frankly, the rat population of the world is staggering, and J. B. S. Haldane, whose essay, 'Man's Destiny', caused considerable alarm in the 1930s, predicted that within a century or so the rat would become a very serious competitor for man's dominion over the earth's surface. Alarming hauls of rats have been reported. My own record of 1,126 in one day pales beside that of a Monsieur Dusaisois, who, in 1840, using makeshift traps, caught 16,050 rats in a month at the awful Monfançon abattoir in France. This slaughterhouse, which specialized in horse knackering, held an incredible quantity of rats – so many, in fact, that it was nearly impossible to walk across the surrounding land without the rat-excavated kennels collapsing. Twigg, in his masterly book *The Brown Rat*, states that it would be impossible to find such conditions today. Perhaps so, but I know of many places which approximate to these conditions, and, macabre as it may seem, as a hunter I am rather pleased that such places still exist, rats having given me incredible sport.

By the 1850s, the effect of the earlier abolition of dog fighting had switched the public interest towards the macabre spectacle known as the rat pits, vividly described in Henry Mayhew's *London Labour and the London Poor*, for there a hundred, sometimes even a thousand, rats would be tipped into a pit and a terrier required to slaughter the pitiful wretches against the clock. Incredible records were recorded, and it required quite a dog to face a mound of a quarter of a ton of

The author with his ratting team – a team that took 3 tons of rats in 1977.

rats and to set about slaying the entire batch. Funnily enough, in spite of the outlawing of such barbarous sports as bull baiting and dog fighting in 1835, the rat pits remained a fairly acceptable sort of sport until 1911, when an Act was passed outlawing the activity. In 1912, the RSPCA successfully prosecuted a notorious Leicester rat-pit owner, a prosecution which brought about the cessation of this timed carnage.

The rat is a fearsome opponent and does not deserve the reputation he has for cowardice. True, he is small in size, and few exceed 12 ounces in weight, but his biting power is phenomenal and the lower incisors can inflict amazingly wide and deep wounds. Few rats readily seek trouble with dogs or cats, but, when pushed and provoked to fight, will usually give an excellent account of themselves. Examine the lacerations on elderly farm cats, note the number of ferrets who refuse to face rats, and look for no further proof of his fighting ability. Rawden Lee, in his book *Terriers*, states that many dogs, and confirmed brawlers and bullies at that, will turn tail and flee when a rat puts in a bite on their noses. Hence the beginner with his puppy will do well to disregard terrier men who tell them that a rat proves no opponent even for a young dog. Such men have probably never hunted rats – and certainly have never caught them in number.

37

Value the sporting qualities of the rat very highly indeed: he will be the last quarry that the anti-field-sport people will seek to protect.

Clearly the rat is too formidable an opponent for the babe with milk teeth still in his gums. Personally, I like to wait until a puppy is eight or nine months of age before I enter him to rat, but there are exceptions to every rule. In 1969, I bred an attractive bitch puppy called Set who proved a real demon at rat hunting. During the bad rains of that winter, most of the rat warrens in my district were flooded and rats were to be found wandering abroad in daylight. This is a fairly uncommon situation, for rats are largely nocturnal by nature. Set chanced upon one of these wanderers, a huge buck, when she was a mite of fourteen weeks, and after a fearful struggle managed to slay the buck. It was the making of Set, though I should add that her sister, Ruach, an excellent ratter when mature, refused to try for rat until she was ten months old. Her haul of rats, however, eventually exceeded that of her illustrious sister. Frankly, I feel Set would have made an even better ratter had she first met up with a rat when she was a great deal older. As I have hinted, premature entering ruins far more terriers than it makes. Only a fool will deliberately encourage a milk-toothed puppy to take on an adult rat, but fools abound among hunters, which accounts for the number of ruined terriers in the temporary hands of dealers.

This is the point to harp back to the question of inoculation once again. It is absolutely essential to inoculate a dog which is to be used for rat hunting. Rats are vile beasts, and they carry an alarming number of diseases, the most dangerous of which is leptospiral jaundice. An uninoculated dog who is bitten by an infected rat, or who licks where an infected rat has urinated, will have little or no chance of surviving the disease. Furthermore, not only does the dog take many months to recover from the disease in the unlikely event of it recovering at all, but it will continue to pass the bacillus in its urine for months after the infection has apparently cleared. Leptospiral jaundice is also highly dangerous to humans, causing an often fatal illness known as Weil's disease – the disease that was the bane of the Victorian rat catchers.

Having assessed the opponent and his fighting quality, the problem is how to engage him and, if possible, kill him. First, dispense with the idea of entering your terrier by placing him in a barrel or shed with a live rat. This is a disastrous method of entering a terrier, which ruins far more terriers than it makes. I have explained the supposed psychology of this method more than adequately in *The Working Terrier*, so will here refrain from repeating myself. Sufficient to say that such a method of entering is the hallmark of the amateur trainer.

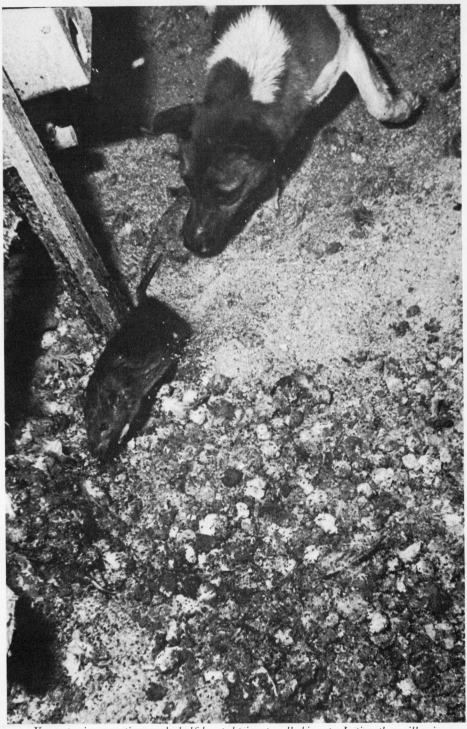

Young terriers sometimes make half-hearted tries at really big rats. In time they will gain confidence and learn to deal with even the biggest bucks.

The problems of ratting two terriers together (as explained in the chapter on quarry) could not be better demonstrated than by examining this unique photograph. Here the rat has been grabbed by one dog and has latched on to another, thereby creating frightful damage.

How, then, should the terrier man start his ward at rat hunting? Well, the simplest if not the best way is to allow the puppy to run with a grown dog – a dog reasonably adept at rat killing. I say reasonably adept, but not too adept, for as Lucas mentions in his book *Hunt and Working Terriers*, an expert rat killer often disparages a puppy (I'll give an illustration of the psychology of this shortly). After a session of watching the adult disposing of rats, the youngster will decide to join in and soon becomes reasonably adept at nabbing rats. This method is not without its weaknesses, however, for rats are rarely killed simply by a terrier nipping them. Most die of spinal dislocation from the shaking given to them by the angry terrier, and some terriers are amazingly adept at dislocating the spines of their victims.

Two dogs rushing in on the same rat also tend to mouth it to death rather than shake it: a singularly ghastly spectacle, and during its death-throes the rat will put in some ferocious work with its teeth. A year or so ago, one of my best bitches ran in on a kill being made by Vampire, my Jack Russell stud dog. Vampire was in the act of shaking the rat when the bitch joined the worry. Before the rat died, he inflicted a deep 3-inch rip on the bitch, a bite that needed stitching.

Fortunately, she was a veteran rat killer, for such a wound would have daunted any puppy.

The next problem is that a puppy ratted alongside an experienced dog will, as he makes a bid at a rat, see the expert snaffle the rat time and time again and become somewhat discouraged at being beaten to the punch every time. Some become so disillusioned that they simply refuse to try for rat when the adult is present. The answer is obvious: rat the puppy by itself until it has regained its confidence. You may lose a few rats by doing so, but it will certainly make the puppy.

I once damned nigh ruined a superb ratting terrier, Drum, by ratting him alongside my best terrier – a veteran called San. At first Drum, who was a precocious puppy, made every effort to catch the rats, but was beaten to the post time and time again by my veteran. After a while, he would simply let the rats run past him, for not only was he a little disillusioned about his lack of ratting aptitude, but he was also slightly afraid of the old dog. I confess I felt inclined to write him off as a failure, but then my veteran was damaged in an affray with a badger and was retired from the ratting team for a month or so. Drum galvanized into life once again and, for a while at least, was one heck of a ratter. When the old dog returned, he went back to being his old self again. Poor old Drum, a heck of a good hunter and a really loyal dog. I eventually lost him after he leaped out of my van into the path of a sports car. It ran him over and broke his back, and the college-scarfed driver never bothered to stop. Shades of Isadora Duncan flashed through my mind, I have to admit.

Where entering is concerned, however, perhaps the best method of them all is the self-entering method. Quite simply, take your puppy to a spot where rats are known to abound and let him set about them in his own sweet time. Sooner or later the babe will make a try for the rats, and after repeated misses will eventually connect and kill. Thus he will become a keen, enthusiastic ratter, all at his own pace. It is a lengthy method of entering, or, rather, it can be, unless one knows about a vast number of rats, but it is certainly one of the best and most natural methods, and is also the way in which wild canines learn to hunt. Not only does it create a properly entered dog, but it also allows the owner a chance to develop what is loosely termed 'bush-craft' – a knowledge of the quarry he is hunting, which is, sadly, a rare quality among hunters today. In time, both hunter and terrier will begin to realize that the rat is vastly overrated as to its intelligence quotient, and always runs well-defined routes between its feeding area and lair. All one therefore needs to do to take rats efficiently is intercept them *en route*. Self-entering also teaches a quality called stealth, a quality without which few rat hunters will be in any way successful, for rat hunting requires a great deal more skill, bush-craft and knowledge of the quarry than any other form of terrier work. It has rightly been said that, to be at all successful, a rat hunt should be conducted as a military manoeuvre.

The best time, nay the only time, to catch rats out feeding is dusk, for the rat is nocturnal. Only diseased or poisoned rats seem to feed during daylight hours. Warfarin – still quite effective in most regions, in spite of what the more alarmist elements of the press have told us – creates a rather disorientated rat, relatively indifferent to the dangers that daylight brings. Most rats found wandering abroad during day-light are probably doped with Warfarin (for this reason, I never feed road casualty rats to my ferrets).

Battery poultry houses, fitted with time switches which plunge the sheds into darkness from time to time, are usually superb places to rat. First you must block the exits (see further detail on the tech-niques below), then allow the shed to remain in darkness for a matter of a few hours, flick on the switch, and away goes the terrier, creating carnage among the fleeing rats. I know of no sport as exciting, and have friends who will come from as far afield as Germany for a good night's ratting. In 1977, I took a haul of three tons of rats simply by ratting poultry sheds. Very few farms are rat free, and, provided the hunter does no damage, ratting places are usually fairly easily obtained.

Of course, to obtain good hauls of rats, meaning very large quanti-ties of rats, one needs to persuade them to leave the security of their holes. This can be done in various ways. Rats may be flooded out by attaching a hose to a tap and inserting the hose into a rat hole. I've had some excellent hauls, flushing rats from concrete piggeries using this method, but it isn't effective against rats which have decided to nest among the rubble or gritty earth that will absorb literally tons of water. Rats can sometimes be shifted from such places by attaching a length of hose to a car exhaust and running the engine with the choke out, so pumping the fumes down the rat hole – not an entirely satisfactory method, since dogs required to work rats in these conditions usually lose all sense of smell for the rest of the day. Perhaps the best method of flushing rats is with ferrets, provided the dog has been broken to ferret, and provided one knows a little about the science of ferreting rats – and a science it is, believe me.

To begin with, the rat is a formidable opponent for the ferret. Not only is it of similar weight (jill ferrets alone can be used for ratting – a hob is much too big to enter an average-sized earth), but a rat can bite as hard as a ferret, and can certainly inflict more serious wounds. Ferrets bitten by rats invariably fester unless treated with antiseptics and antibiotics, and while I must admit I've never actually seen a rat

42

kill a ferret, I have buried countless good jills that have died as a result of rat bites. I buried my very best sandy jill a few days before writing this chapter – a victim of quite a minor rat bite. Minor? Well, not quite, for she died three days after being bitten. Furthermore, it is a mistake to imagine that all the rats immediately race screaming out of a warren at the merest whiff of a ferret. Remember this when you see your ferret backing out from a warren, tail in a gale, driven before the onslaught of a furious rat. In the winter time, when there is little or no breeding going on, the chances are that your rats will bolt hell-for-leather. Summer ferreting in warrens where breeding activity is at its peak is, however, a different matter. A doe with a litter of young-sters able to fend for themselves will certainly bolt, the devil taking the hindmost of her babes. But one with a helpless litter, or, worse still, with a recently drawn nest, will usually defy even the most valiant ferret. One with a newly made nest is a positive heller, and I've seen does heavy in young follow a ferret out of a warren and attack it savagely in the open. I took a photograph of one such inci-dent at Mexborough.

Sooner or later, a jill comes to realize that the rat warren is thwart with dangers and will simply quit rat hunting. There is no magical way of getting her to re-enter to rat. She has simply had enough. If she receives a mauling while still immature, she will quit early; if she is very lucky and doesn't take a hiding until she is four or five years of age (and lucky she will need to be to go so long without a beating), she will sooner or later run up against an opponent who is too much for her and decide she has had enough. In a lifetime of hunting rats, and hunting them with almost lunatic regularity, I have only once owned a jill that went on to rat to the end of her days. She was ex-tremely lucky until, at eight years old, she took a bad bite beneath the eye, from which she subsequently died. I valued her greatly, my entire ferretry being inbred to this little gladiator, but I have bred none to equal the records of the old matron. Thus it is obvious that, to hunt rats properly and frequently, should you be lucky enough to find good ratting locations, you will require a large stock of jills, and maybe a dozen is not too many. The cost of keeping such a predatory menagerie? Well, so long as you are ratting regularly it need not be high, for the flesh of rat makes good and nourishing ferret food. If you live in a built-up area though, you could well have a problem feeding rats to your ferrets, but then keeping a dozen ferrets will usually make a man fairly immune to the complaints of neighbours in any case.

The time has come to get your terrier familiarized with the ferrets – to such a degree that he will drink from the same dish without either party attacking the other. This familiarity is necessary, for not only will the terrier develop a healthy respect for the ferret, it will also be able to make snap decisions about the nature of the creature emerging at speed from the rat warren. Terriers trained in this manner rarely mouth or hurt a ferret. Is there a small disadvantage to such familiarity? Yes, because ferrets and dogs can both die from distemper and it can be communicated from dog to ferret. I inoculate my ferrets against distemper, so have little problem with the effects of this disease. The precaution can be carried out very cheaply, so long as you can persuade your vet to split a vaccine; one dose of canine distemper vaccine is usually enough to inoculate between five and ten ferrets. I've used a Canilep ampule to inoculate twenty ferrets, and not one died when distemper wiped out all other local ferrets.

Now, to hunt your new-formed team of man, dog and ferret will be a fairly simple matter, providing you know something about rat behaviour and are prepared to conduct a hunt like a military manoeuvre. First, visit the area you intend to hunt. The presence of rats should be fairly obvious, with well-beaten tracks leading between their holes and feeding grounds. Place a few obstacles across the main pathway: a brick, a bale of straw, a branch, anything that could cause the rat to check its flight and give the terrier a slight advantage. Next check the main holes and note any carefully concealed bolt-holes, bolt-holes so inconspicuous that rats can sneak out of them without so much as making a sound. Block one or two of the most tricky ones: those under hedges, those nearest to unblockable drains. Next check your terrain and make sure that all hiding places, to where a rat could flash in times of trouble, are blocked. Unsporting, you say? All right, but disregard this advice and your haul will be negligible or frankly nil. *Rattus norwegicus* has not survived two hundred years of savage persecution by being sporting enough to give a dog a fair chance of nailing him. Furthermore, few rats move outside the half-acre surrounding their lairs, and most spend their lives dashing 'twixt lair and feeding ground. Thus they know every square inch of their terrain and make use of any place they can hide when danger threatens. The chances of catching rats without adopting such unsporting measures as blocking and confusing the rat are therefore quite small. Furthermore, if after being invited to hunt a farm to clear it of rats you manage to spend only a thoroughly sporting but fruitless day as the rats sneak 'twixt bales and rubbish, eluding both dog and ferret, then naturally your farmer friend will be a little doubtful as to your hunting ability and may decide that poison is a better method of controlling rats than inviting this very sporting idiot and his dogs.

Forget sportsmanship when clearing rats and have no worries about wiping out an entire colony – conservation is not the problem

Rat hunting is a military manoeuvre if conducted properly. If holes are not blocked prior to a hunt few or no rats will be taken. An unblocked area will be an escape route for a horde of rats.

A correctly blocked exit. Contrast this scene with scene A.

of the rat hunter. If a food supply exists, and it's bound to, otherwise the colony wouldn't be around on the farm in the first place, then a matter of only a few weeks will see other rats moving in to fill the ecological vacuum. A few months will see a new, thriving colony, creating the same carnage as before. Have no fear of it, and, as a well-organized rat hunter with a steady team of terriers, you will never be out of sport. Britain holds a population of nearly fifty million rats, all foul, all verminous and most of them a storehouse of all the deadly infections known to man. *Rattus norwegicus* has no place in Britain, but he would be impossible to eradicate completely.

What a damnable hypocrite I am, for no animal has given me such sport. I hunted one poultry farm for a whole year, every night of the year, apart from a month I spent in hospital with rat-bite fever, and took a staggering haul of rats. After a year of hunting, my dogs looked like advertisements for mange compounds – the before shot, not the after. They were so scabied that they had to be sent to a Yorkshire kennel to recuperate. And I scarcely made an inroad into that rat population. The rat is the greatest filler of an ecological vacuum. Sufficient to say, the present writer has hunted rats for thirty-four years and classes himself as quite an efficient hunter. Yet I have never, ever, totally eradicated the rats on any one farm.

Enough of the ethics of rat hunting – now to take them. Having cleared the decks for action, allow maybe an hour for the rat, alerted by all the bustle above ground, to calm down. Back now quickly, dog on slip or held by collar. Insert the ferret into a likely hole and watch the ferret closely; she'll tell you much about the contents of the hole. As she enters the alien and often hostile confines of the lair, her tail may become like a bottle brush, or it may lash from side to side like an angry cat's. Let her alone now, and don't push her in towards the waiting rats. She will go in in her own good time. Tail lashing is a fair indication that the rat is at home, for ferrets, unlike dogs, are rarely false markers. After all, it is difficult to over-encourage a ferret – the cause of false marking in most dogs. Hold the dog now, don't allow him to sniff his presence down the hole. The name of the game is to persuade the rat that the hostile world above ground is far more welcoming than the creature harassing him below ground. In a few moments, your ferret will find her rat and begin to persuade it to seek the sanctuary of the surface.

The rat bolts, and bolting rats can clock up to 24 m.p.h. over a yard or so. Slip the frenzied dog and, if your blocking has been professional, you will get your rat. Don't move yet awhile. Rats rarely live solitary lives, and where there is one there is a chance there are others. Stop your terrier ragging the body of the rat, but not so harshly as to make

This incredible photograph is of probably the largest rat ever taken, a giant of 2lbs 4 ounces. It is certainly the largest live rat ever photographed.

A first class ratting terrier is a tremendous athlete. Here the author's Omega is shown taking a leaping rat.

him think he has done wrong by killing the rat. Like as not there will be more work for him in a moment or so – and there is. The writer's best ferreted haul was 710 in a day, but the reader should bear in mind the fact that many, many ferrets were badly bitten during this day's work and that the place where this haul was taken had been keepered for months before the hunt. I am actually lunatic enough to ensure that my rats are not disturbed before a major hunt.

Hauls on this scale are, of course, rare, but a great deal of sport can be had from catching maybe half a dozen or so rats in piggeries or poultry houses. Let the purist terrier man scoff – his untrained terriers on a leash as like as not – that ferreting and ratting are minor sports and he is concerned only with badger and fox digging. Fool that he is. He will get very little sport if his dogs are trained only to this narrow spectrum of quarry. But you, with your ferrets and ratting terriers, will find sport aplenty on tips, farms and rubbish dumps, for the fickle fur market has since 1977 made foxes quite scarce, but rats, well, they are still abundant, and long may the terrier man find them so.

The Stoat and the Mink

Time presses me now to leave my favourite quarry and to pass on to the pursuit of a far less common creature, the stoat; and, for purpose of convenience, it will be expedient to include the mink alongside this valiant little animal. Both are members of a large family called the mustelids, a group of creatures famed for their courage and utter recklessness. Badgers, otters and wolverines are members of this group, as is the diminutive lesser weasel. Oddly enough, as a family it is characterized by an almost insane blood lust. One has only to lose a ferret (a member of the same family) near a poultry house to discover the awful truth of this statement in the carnage that will result. Stoats are, perhaps, not as bloodthirsty as ferrets, even though bloodthirsty is hardly a term one should scientifically apply to animals. But stoats, too, can cause a fair degree of damage during a night's rampage.

At the end of the 1960s, I reared a batch of Khaki Campbell ducklings to produce eggs to feed my crop of puppies. After ensuring that the area around the cottage was free of rats, for rats are absolute demons at duckling killing, I set off to the New Forest one weekend to hunt stoat with my pack of terriers. When I returned it was to find that a stoat had taken up residence in a near-by rabbit warren and had made murderous inroads into my crop of ducks. A sad indictment on a man reputed to be a hunter – 'physician heal thyself' may seem an apt comment here, perhaps.

Mink are equally destructive, and besides being extremely fast and agile, they can swim like otters. Mink, unlike the stoat, are not native to Britain, though I believe that a species of mink may once have been indigenous to our country. Those at present loose in the countryside are simply descendants of escapees from mink farms. So great is the damage done by these feral mink, originally natives of Canada, that it has become extremely difficult to get planning permission to start a mink farm, and no licence will be granted to breed mink unless the premises are highly secure and escape proof. Incidentally, it seems likely that, after a recent horrific happening concerning a child who was killed by ferrets, the ferret may also become a licensed animal just like the mink, though it will be extremely interesting to see how the powers-that-be propose to enforce such licensing laws on the hosts of itinerants who seem to be regular losers of ferrets in the district where I live. But then itinerants are subject to very few laws in our somewhat paradoxical country.

To return to mink, however, they are a number-one nuisance to water birds and other river dwellers and indulge in orgies of destruction whenever they can. Besides having the destructive, all-consuming killing instinct of the ferret, they are also one of the fastest creatures ever likely to be encountered. At one mink farm where I spent a great deal of time, for my interest in mustelids was for a while close to fascination, I once saw a small rat run across the top of the mink cage above a sleeping mink, which promptly galvanized into action and pulled the rat through the bars of the cage. The whole incident, from the start of deep sleep, for mustelids sleep very deeply indeed, to the catching of the rat and its dismembering, took less than a second. This lightning-quick response to the catching of prey and also in attack is well worth bearing in mind when hunting this quarry – a quarry which, I should add, can inflict wounds on a dog quite out of proportion to its diminutive size.

In the last few years, otter hunting has become illegal in England and Wales, and many otter hound packs have been given a reprieve, somewhat temporary, I should like to wager, to allow them to hunt mink. Terrier packs, or even small teams of terriers, will hunt mink equally as well, however, and certainly more efficiently I would claim. Yet, in spite of hunting, the mink seems to be on the increase, for few of the problems which plague the breeder of high-density levels of domesticated mink seem to bother it in the wild. Perhaps the diseases which cause the death of many mink, such as Aleutian disease and botulism, are a result of contributory factors brought

49

about by keeping solitary beasts in unnatural, overcrowded conditions. It would be of interest to discover whether wild mink ever suffer from botulism or Aleutian disease.

Stoats once abounded in Britain. Prior to the introduction of myxomatosis into the country and the subsequent reduction of the rabbit population, stoats were very numerous indeed, living, as they did, on rabbit. However, a survey undertaken by a team of naturalists in 1960 placed the stoat on the outer fringes of the endangered British species list. Many stoats, driven by hunger after the rabbit had begun to die off, were found in rubbish dumps hunting young rats; but while a baby grey rat is fairly easy meat for a stoat, an adult buck, or a doe drawing her nesting bedding, is usually capable of putting all but the hungriest and most foolhardy stoat to flight. I have watched several battles between rat and stoat, and in spite of children's story-book tales to the contrary, have never yet seen an adult rat bested by a stoat. Henry Williamson, author of *Tarka the Otter*, who, along with Maurice Burton, must rank as one of the finest naturalists who ever drew breath, once told me that he had seen an adult buck rat, as hoary and scabrous as most patriarchal rats, deliberately police his harem of does against the ravages of a colony of stoats who lived in a near-by hedgerow, even venturing into the lairs of the stoats to do battle with them. Marais made the same observations about baboons and leopards. Truly, terrier men have much to learn from naturalists of this calibre.

Now that the rabbit population is increasing again, there is little doubt that the stoat will make a comeback, but the rat, which is an unnatural diet for the stoat, would not have sustained these predators for much longer I fear.

But to the hunting of these creatures. Stoats are still fairly plentiful in districts where rabbits are numerous, and they can usually be caught out hunting during the evenings or early mornings. Few terriers are overmatched by a stoat, which is only the size of a medium-sized jill ferret, but killing one is one thing, catching one quite another. Quicksilver is the only word to describe the stoat. Many times I have seen excellent rat killers – dogs capable of almost acrobatic skills when catching rats – hopelessly outrun, outclassed and dazzled by the incredible agility of the stoat. A few months before the time of writing, I began to hunt a stoat that had taken up residence in a grove of scrub oak and alder interlaced with bramble just a hundred yards from the house. In spite of morning and evening runs at him with my team of yearling terriers, he is still, as I write this, unharmed. Do not be surprised to see stoats escaping almost certain death by lightning-quick movements when a terrier's jaws are literally a hair's breadth from being clamped on the stoat's body. Nothing increases a dog's speed of response, his awareness to lightning-quick movements of quarry, like stoat hunting. After hunting stoat for a while, however, many dogs seem to learn to anticipate a stoat's erratic looping run and learn to catch them moderately easily, even as a lurcher run regularly at hare becomes dextrous at anticipating the hare's twists and turns. During 1978, while ferreting a bank at my village, two stoats skipped my rabbit nets and bolted, and Omega, my most athletic terrier, collared both before they went ten yards from my nets.

Stoat hunting is fast, furious and excellent sport, for not only is the stoat agile and nimble, he is also able to climb quite well; and while not so much at home in the branches as his cousin the pine marten, he will use trees to his advantage when he is hard pressed. Gladdish Hulkes, a famous stoat hunter of the New Forest during the early part of the century, kept a pack of Sealyhams exclusively to hunt stoat (though it is said that they would always riot on rabbit), and he achieved not only good hauls, but also the enthusiastic support of his small field, surviving members of which still recall with great nostalgia the chase with this excellent hunter (who was again a superb naturalist) who hunted this most elusive quarry.

Stoats are usually quite easily bolted with ferrets, and will rarely make a fight of it with their smelly kin bloods. Should the stoat be prepared to make a stand, however, watch out for squalls. About a year ago I was hunting a bank behind a poultry farm, a spot famous for rats (I'd taken 110 only a few weeks before). The location proved ratless, however, and the ferrets weaved in and out of the empty warrens and tested the edges, as a ferret is wont to do in a warren only recently vacated. I was just a little perplexed as to why the cupboard should suddenly be bare, for, over the previous ten years, I had always had good sport ratting this bank. Then, halfway down the bank, I saw a greyish, brown body flash between the rat lairs and realized why the previous tenants were no longer at home.

Rats will, when pushed, easily get the better of a fully grown stoat and deal him such wounds that, for ever after, it will give them a clear berth. Let a stoat take refuge in the warren, however, and it becomes a different tale. Rats are unassuming creatures and vacate a warren in winter (in summer, things are different) rather than chance a battle with a stoat or weasel. Possibly also the breeding cycle of rat does is disturbed by the presence of an arch-predator, much as monkeys are reputed not to breed if they are caged in permanent view of a cage of large predatory felines. Enough, however, of hypotheses. The fact was that a stoat was in possession of the warren. My dogs became almost paralysed, frozen with anticipation as I put the oldest sandy jill ferret I had into the lair. She flashed into action, tail lashing and hissing like a cat. All hell broke loose, and the earth became impregnated with a mixture of musteline smells. The stoat flashed out, and Beltane, my oldest Jack Russell terrier, chopped at him. Stoats have an amazing gift of being able to arrest in flight, almost in mid-air, doubling back on themselves like a medieval tumbler. The old bitch missed by a foot. Almost as fast as an arrow, the stoat shot back down the hole, this time prepared to face and fight the ferret.

Now, most stoats will bolt time and time again against a ferret, but, sure as damn it, if you make a rule about animals, the very next of the species you encounter will be the first to break the rule. For ten minutes the screaming battle 'twixt ferret and stoat took place, and my dogs went wild with excitement and had to be restrained. At last my jill emerged, a mass of punctures. Common sense will tell a hunter when to give the quarry best, and I left the stoat unharmed. My jill died the next day. Most stoats bolt, however, and likewise most stoats die from a single chop by a terrier, and, for that matter, so do most ferrets – to emphasize a warning that cannot be too often repeated, tiro terrier man.

I confess I am a relative newcomer to mink hunting, and only since the publication of my book *The Working Terrier*, in which I confessed I had done very little hunting of mink, have I actually taken part in serious organized mink hunting. For this I have to thank the honesty of my earlier book, for I've been inundated with invitations to hunt mink. Most mink stay close to water, living, as they do, on fish, water fowl and amphibians. Any dog who intends to take on mink must therefore be prepared to get his feet wet, and a sight more of his anatomy as well. Border terriers, and Russells with considerable Border terrier blood, are usually wonderfully aquatic and make excellent mink-hunting dogs. Furthermore, though it requires a dog with a very good nose to work rat along brooks – for rats are, in spite of their reputation for being fairly filthy, scentless – the mink, particularly those pursued, are remarkably easy to trail. When mustelids of all sorts are upset, angry, or even off-country, their scent glands explode or leak. Even a man would then be able to trail one with a modicum of success. Eddie Chapman, once terrier man for the Monmouthshire Hunt, though now I understand terrier man for the Avon Vale Hunt, had some excellent runs at mink, and in spite of the fact that hauls are unlikely to be large (mink are not sociable animals, and live solitary existences) the sport is quite exceptional and exhilarating.

The Coypu

Coypu can give considerable sport for some, though, I confess, not for me. These are huge rat-like beasts which formerly escaped (though deliberately released would probably be more accurate) from fur farms, perhaps in the hope that they would provide a ready stock of wild, saleable furs. Gradually, they colonized the fens and the Norfolk Broads. Some male coypus are extremely large – 25 pounds is not unknown – but they are hardly the fighters one would expect from 25-pound rat-like creatures. Wounds inflicted by battling coypu are usually superficial and heal easily. Sometimes, however, large fragments of their bright-orange chisel-like teeth remain in a wound and cause sepsis. One vet dug out a half-inch piece of incisor from a terrier. During the early 1960s, society, prompted by ill-informed newspaper articles, became decidedly uptight about the thought of coypu colonizing Britain and duplicating the problem which the musk rat became in the 1930s. Two coypu were killed by the Crowhurst Otter Hounds in Sussex in 1950, and by 1960 the Ministry of Agriculture estimated that 200,000 of these curious creatures were living wild in Britain. Britain promptly took up arms against this creature, which resembled nothing so much as an ill-fated H. G. Wells' experiment, and trappers and terrier men descended on the ugly beasts with the total extermination of the species as their objective. The state paid out £75,500 for the pogrom, pogrom being the operative word, I feel, and a staggering total of 40,461 coypu was taken.

This was, I always felt, a totally unnecessary slaughter. As it happened, the harsh winter of 1963 saw off thousands of these gentle rodents, and probably far more than the Ministry of Agriculture campaign against them did. The coypu, being a native of the semi-tropical regions of South America, must have suffered greatly in the severity of the 1963 winter, which must have had a tremendous impact on a creature bred only to endure a mild climate. Since then, the coypu has never recovered its original numbers. It is doubtful whether this beast will become totally extinct in Britain until industrialization drains and poisons the Broads, but it is also unlikely it will ever become the plague that the newspapers believed it would.

Coypu are easily taken and bolt quite easily to terriers. They can be netted, though their bolt-holes are usually below the waterline, but they are usually best shot, or else the escape holes blocked before being dug with the aid of terriers. The excavation of a fully grown coypu is staggering in its dimensions, and waterways have actually altered course because of the undermining of the banks by coypu.

Frankly, though I took many in the years between 1962 and 1968, I do not, as I say, enjoy hunting these beasts, and find the sight of one timidly 'backing' a baying terrier, the coypu splintering its orange teeth in terror, a sight that induces pity and nausea.

In spite of the fact that the coypu is not considered to be a really formidable opponent for the working terrier, terriers should have considerable experience tackling other quarry before entering to coypu. Not only does the coypu weigh in at over a stone, but the terrier is forced to encounter them in sets or earths which are sometimes half-filled with water, and while it is expected that the terrier should give a good account of itself against any vermin, it is a little unfair to try a tiro terrier to coypu and expect the dog to do well. Also, it should be kept in mind that it is essential to spend time hunting a fair number of rats or stoat before considering launching the puppy against heavier, more dangerous quarry.

The Fox

Recently, when I judged a show in South Wales, I heard the familiar bleat of a disillusioned terrier man saying, 'Don't know why he's failed fox. I gave him a rat or two and then tried him, and he backed down to Charlie' – he was talking about a dog which was just seven months old! As a general principle, one should always hunt a puppy regularly to quarry that will not overtax him. (Once, at a time when I specialized in training ruined dogs, I spent five months trying a failed terrier puppy on voles found beneath galvanized sheets alongside the canal side in Rotherham.) This constant and regular hunting not only enables the puppy to gain experience of hunting to test his steel on suitable quarry, but it allows the dog to develop a link between him and his owner, a link as old as canine domestication itself, a link that can never be forged between dogs and the man who buys trained dogs, or the man who is in feverish haste to try his dog at large quarry. Which brings us to the staple quarry of the terrier: namely, the fox.

Let us begin with the straight truth. Foxes are formidable foes, so the would-be terrier man will do well to disregard the fool who tells him that there are terriers who dispose of foxes in seconds, killing them as deftly as a trained dog slays rats. Before believing such misleading and inane tales, the hunter should examine the lacerations on terriers which work regularly with hound packs. Few dogs who see regular service with hounds are not without fearful scars, and fewer still are the terriers who are without loss of teeth as a result of awesome tussles with foxes. My best fox-hunting terrier saw combat

The Monmouthshire Hunt Terrier man with his useful well-matched team. Eddie Chapman was one of the founder members of the Jack Russell Club of Great Britain.

with several hundred foxes, and by the age of eight there was little of his face which was not entirely composed of scar tissue. You have only to examine some of the Fell terriers at hunt shows. They are usually very hard, tough little dogs, bred for the task not only of being capable of bolting a fox, but also of killing him should he decide not to bolt. Many of them have had their jaws broken or twisted out of alignment as a result of battles with foxes. In the light of this, consider now the fool who airily dismisses the fox as a quarry that can be slain as easily as a rat. 'Foe' would describe the fox rather than 'quarry', for the result of a duel 'twixt dog and fox can easily go either way – ask any fell hunter how many plucky little terriers he has buried as a result of conflicts with foxes. Also, bear in mind that a terrier which has taken rat or stoat will have killed them above ground in daylight, or at least during twilight. He is now required to go into the lair of the fox and fight him, or bay at him, in the total darkness – darkness which the fox is quite accustomed to. Furthermore, the dog must face his foe in earths which are often filled with noxious gases such as methane, or a high level of carbon dioxide as a result of root decay – conditions to which a fox is well accustomed, but which are totally foreign to the terrier.

Logically, it is too much to expect a callow youngster, a puppy, to face such a foe, but the number of hunters who enter puppies prematurely is consistently frightening. Many men boast of having entered puppies at six months to fox. Only the day before writing this, I heard a local hunter state that his six-month-old puppy was already a demon to badger but wouldn't look at a fox. Make no mistake, some puppies will go to fox as babes, in the same way that a teenage lad would consider taking on Mohammed Ali after the exhilaration of a dance or a night out – and the result would be comparable, believe me. Premature entering to any quarry has a disastrous effect on the terrier's mental make-up. The puppy (or the youth) will receive a severe thrashing and refuse to consider further contest with the quarry that has bested him.

Incidentally, these victims will as a rule be the 'just started' puppies you are usually offered by dealers. While there are puppies which will enter to foxes like tigers, these are usually finished or ruined by the time they have seen their first birthday, and again they pass into the hands of dealers who specialize in selling entered dogs. Premature entering is never advisable, and frankly will have a deleterious effect on the further hunting efficiency of any hunting dog. It would be untrue for me to say that I have never tried puppies to fox, for it is a terrible temptation to try a flyer to heavy quarry – a flyer chafing at the bit to engage the fox – but, no matter how much the terrier man wishes to test the mettle of his puppy, he should refrain from trying him. Some of the most famous hunt terriers ever were, after all, remarkably slow at entering, some only entering to fox at three or four years of age. Cobby's dog, Pincher, a superb dog by anyone's standards – the number of bitches he covered bore witness to the fact – was four before he really became wed to fox hunting.

Brian Forsyth of the Warwickshire Hunt, a man who justly has a reputation for hardly ever failing with a dog and who can really and truly boast that he is an authority on working terriers, once had a dog who was a renowned worker, yet it would not even consider tackling a fox until it was well into its third season. Forsyth persevered with the dog where many would have passed him on or simply put him down, and the animal has become a near legend in the Warwickshire Hunt country. The dog may not have begun work until he was three, but thereafter Forsyth still worked him and worked him hard into his tenth year, and no dog justified Forsyth's patience more.

If the reader still needs convincing of the folly of premature entering, there is one more tale to tell. The Robson family of the Border Hunt bred a type of terrier we now know as the Border terrier. These terriers are remarkably slow to enter, for they usually stay both timid and infantile until well into adulthood. The Robsons claimed that they never intentionally set out to enter a terrier, and I have no doubt that this is true. Their terriers were allowed to run with the hounds and watch a fox put to ground. When they were good and ready – and it was the terrier who decided this state of readiness, not the huntsman – they went to fox. One of the Robson's terriers, a dog called Flint (a common name with Borders), was supposedly well into his fifth year before he chanced a joust with a fox. Flint became quite a famous dog in the Border district, and reputedly worked until his sixteenth birthday.

Premature entering is therefore a little pointless and decidedly wasteful. How, then, should we enter a terrier to fox? In a nutshell the answer is: when he is ready, and in private. Privacy is most important, as the dog is apt to make a fool of his owner during a first try at fox, and while this is usually forgiven if it happens in private, when it occurs in public, as at a hunt meet, it will as a rule be greeted with hoots of derision (usually from people who have either left a dog at home or who don't even own an entered terrier; it is staggering how many dogless terrier experts abound). Such an incident can have a very damaging effect on the relationship between a man and his dog, damage that can take some time to repair. Wounds of the flesh heal rapidly, but wounds to pride take a great deal longer.

First things first, however. The would-be fox hunter has now completed a goodly spell of rat hunting, the longer the spell the better – a year is not too long – and maybe chopped a few stoats and weasels as well. He has decided the dog is ready for his first tilt at fox, and the dog should be about eighteen months old before he sees his first fox. Time during puppyhood should have been spent wisely, the dog encouraged to run free and hunt up small quarry. He will, if the owner has given him the chance, have explored dry drains, and vanished into empty earths – don't over-encourage him in this activity, incidentally. He will have explored cavities in the ground for the myriad exciting scents that linger there.

All these things he should have done, though he should not have been over-encouraged in any of them. A dog 'looed' into every earth the owner finds will almost certainly be only too glad to please his owner by diving into every earth he sees and probably giving tongue in excitement. In this over-enthusiasm is born the malady known as false marking, for such a dog will eventually give tongue in any empty earth, believing that he is pleasing his master by doing so. Once this habit has begun, it is the very devil to break, and I know of no really effective, hundred per cent certain method of breaking it. But never-

57

theless the dog should be acquainted with the act of going into the bowels of the earth to seek its prey.

One word of advice, however, before we proceed further. Rabbits invariably cohabit with foxes, a statement that may seem a little incongruous at first, but which, on examination, is fairly logical. Foxes in search of new earths usually find inhabited rabbit burrows and enlarge them for their own use, the rabbits then living in a state of uneasy tenancy with the main chambers of the warren inhabited by foxes. Now, terriers usually take to rabbit hunting fairly readily, for rabbits have a sweet, almost pungent scent that dogs invariably find irresistible – far more exciting to them than the scent of fox, in fact, for the fox is not a natural quarry of dogs of any breed. But dogs that are not steady to rabbit – which, in hunting terminology, means dogs that will hunt rabbit – will on occasions leave their legitimate quarry (and, by legitimate, I mean fox or badger) to dig to a rabbit – an annoying habit that reduces the value of the terrier. I have often spent hours digging to friends' terriers, dogs which their owners assured me were totally steady to rabbit, only to find the dog baying at a bunny in one of the myriad tunnels that criss-cross every established warren. Furthermore, a rabbit is able to squeeze into a tiny crack, so the terrier often digs to get to his prey and subsequently walls himself in the earth, shutting off the air supply and subsequently dying for his interest in rabbits. Many dogs are certainly trapped and suffocated by working to fox, but rabbits claim a far more substantial number of terrier victims than do foxes – an incongruous-seeming statement, perhaps, but true.

Cobby once told me that, in pre-war days, long before myxomatosis reduced the rabbit to a rarity, some rabbit warrens were so large and so ancient that they resembled a labyrinth. In 1919, my father's two drinking partners, a pair of Welsh miners, dug for eight days in a Carmarthenshire rabbit warren to extract a terrier that had become trapped fifteen feet below ground. Such enormous warrens have become rare since myxomatosis reduced the rabbit population, but there are still many that will trap a terrier. Dogs intended for serious fox hunting, meaning dogs required either to work only fox for hunts or as vermin exterminators, should be stock steady to rabbit.

The trick is usually taught by allowing a few wild rabbits (tame rabbits have a totally different scent, it appears) to run in an enclosure, the terrier puppy who makes a try at them then being chastized. Sooner or later, he will learn to accept that rabbits are *verboten* as prey, and he will no longer riot on bunnies. Nimrod Capel's famous dog, Bluecap (1908), was said to be so stock steady with rabbit that he would allow one to eat from his plate, yet he was a demon to fox.

Capel always ensured that all his hunt terriers were steady to rabbit, and he put down any dogs who were keen on running them. Rather a drastic measure for the average rough hunter, perhaps, but Capel used to say that it was a terrier's job to provide sport for the hunting field; and during the golden age of fox hunting, a time where hunt service jobs were ranked as relatively well paid and foxes actually keepered, few of the field relished a long wait while a terrier took out his fury on a rabbit, leaving a fox time to dig himself an impregnable fortress below ground. Rabbiting terriers are great fun – I find them so, I must admit – but they're always one heck of a nuisance to serious fox hunters.

But, to return to the task in hand, the terrier is now considered ready for fox. The time for the free-running terrier is at an end. Today he should be leashed, and released only as the owner considers it suitable to do so. So to work, dog on leash. The terrier man finds an earth known to contain foxes, or, at least, that has the reputation for being a 'fox lie-up'. It is also an earth that does not look particularly deep – famous last words, perhaps, for even one-eyed sets can be extraordinarily deep sometimes. I could tell some horrid tales of one such one-eyed set. At all events, the terrier strains at the leash and the earth smells strongly of fox.

Slip the dog. Chances are he will crawl carefully into the earth to explore it; chances are also that the earth will be uninhabited, for foxes dig dozens of earths and abide in them only a night or so before moving on. Favourite earths invariably contain foxes, but many are used for only a night's lodging when the fox is far from home. If the fox is evidently not at home, do not encourage the dog to go back into the earth. Take his word for it that no one is in. Encouraging him to race out of and into the earth will not only make a fool of him, it will encourage the cardinal sin of false marking, as I have just explained. Therefore, try for another earth.

Sooner or later you will connect, and your dog will find his fox at home. But the first encounter with a fox is usually a bit of a puzzle to a terrier, for there is no natural enmity 'twixt dog and fox. It can, it is true, easily be created by allowing the terrier to rag an old fox skin, or, better still, a carcass. I always stop the car to pick up road-casualty foxes for my terriers, and while the man in the street would probably consider me bats for picking up fox carcasses and stowing them in the boot of my car, it certainly helps me to enter a terrier. Take no notice of what people say. The world in general considers the terrier man to be a hopeless lunatic anyway. Few genuine countrymen waste anything.

So, the terrier encounters his first fox and the dog's responses will vary from individual to individual. Some nervy characters give tongue madly. Nervy terriers often make exceptionally good fox-bolting dogs, though nervy dogs often bay at fresh scent after the fox has left. Other more phlegmatic terriers simply give a deep throaty growl. If you are certain the fox is in residence, and, I admit, it is difficult to ascertain this without the use of a trained fox dog, now is the time to shout encouragement to your terrier. Allow him to bay like thunder at the quarry, tease it, savour its pungent, exhilarating odour, before you start digging to the fox. Even more important, allow the dog to drive the fox around the earth, to pin it, fix it, bottle it up in a blind hole before starting to dig. Unsporting as it sounds, it remains more or less essential to kill one's first fox and allow the dog to worry the carcass, particularly if the dog has received a mauling from the fox. Make no mistake about it, the headstrong, aggressive beginner will usually take quite a serious beating from an adult fox. The dog, if he is allowed to worry the carcass, will then feel elated with his victory and be prepared to receive further injuries during later hunts without quitting his fox.

But do kill the fox as quickly and painlessly as possible. Do not allow the dog to worry or rag the still-living body. This is asking for trouble, for not only will the now-desperate fox be able to defend itself mightily and cause fearsome damage to a dog, but such an action has, I believe, a degrading effect on the hunter, if one can call a man who allows a dog to rag a still-living fox a hunter. Allow such barbarism, and you cross the line between the hunter and the baiter, and I know of no more loathsome person than the baiter of wild animals. There is, in spite of public opinion, a considerable difference between the two. Furthermore, such a practice gives magnificent ammunition to the anti-blood-sports brigade. At the present day, the hunting fraternity is under constant fire from this body. To create unnecessary pain in an animal, and it has to be faced that death is never totally painless, no matter what pro-hunting propaganda leads the layman to believe, is merely to beg for trouble. Kill your quarry, and kill it as quickly and painlessly as possible with the minimum theatrical exhibitionism.

Whether or not foxes need exterminating is, of course, a moot point. They can be a nuisance in the countryside, and even more so in a town, but this is probably a consequence of man's interfering stupidity in introducing myxomatosis and reducing the rabbit population. Since the reduction of the rabbit, foxes have changed their feeding habits quite considerably. Forty years ago, a fox in Birmingham's city centre would have merited a letter to *The Times*, but since the decline of the rabbit, scavenging city foxes are so common that they no longer make interesting newspaper copy. These city foxes need sources of meat, though most exist on far more vegetable matter than the 20 per cent animal protein usually stipulated in pre-myxomatosis days. However, they still need small mammals and birds to supplement the high vegetable diet to be obtained by scavenging in a city. Rats provide a large proportion of this protein, and, again, contrary to most theories, rats are the staple diet of most country foxes, while foxes are frequent visitors to ash tips and rubbish dumps to hunt these rodents. When supplies of these fail, look out for squalls. In 1970, Birmingham experienced a real problem regarding its fox population. Reports of poultry, guinea pigs, tame rabbits and even half-grown cats being killed and eaten were almost daily occurrences, and though only a few foxes were seen (foxes are largely nocturnal), they certainly made their presence felt. It was quite amazing how many terrier men appeared within Birmingham itself to deal with the problem – men who would normally have had to travel thirty miles to catch foxes.

Country foxes are not the demons which story books relate. Where rabbits are numerous, little or no damage is done by foxes, and even if the rabbit population dwindles, most foxes will take to living on voles and rats and other small rodents rather than chance their necks by coming near to human habitation to take poultry. In a hard winter, things are different, of course. In 1963, I lived in Shropshire, and that awful winter certainly reduced all forms of wild life to emaciated skeletons. Attacks on my poultry were common. One fox attacked them by daylight hours and refused to be driven away from my holding. For days he circled the poultry pens, making tracks in the deep snow and biting through the wood of the hen house in spite of the furious barking of my kennel terriers. To finish the tale, one night I heard a fearsome battle taking place near my house, and morning found large footprints around the scuffed and bloody snow, in the centre of which lay my fox. One of the lurchers from the local tinker site, a mile from my house (the tinkers having caused me a heck of a sight more trouble than the fox, I must add) must have chanced on the weakened fox and ended him.

Even so, poultry thefts are relatively rare, even in mid-winter, and though hunts try to justify themselves by stating that they keep down raiding foxes, this is far from the truth. Vixens with cubs will sometimes cause havoc, particularly if poultry houses are old and rickety. I once lived near a free-range poultry keeper, a curious type of man who believed, quite rightly, I suppose, that man was poisoning his environment with chemical fertilizers and intensive farming methods. His farm was the most neatly kept I have ever seen, though there were rats aplenty, for he refused to use poison to control them. Hence I spent many happy hours ferreting the property of this curious and fascinating eccentric.

One day he arrived at my cottage with a tale of woe, stating that a vixen and her cubs had slaughtered his entire crop of young pullets and that the scene at his farm resembled an explosion at a feather-mattress factory. A mile from his house was an enormous badger set which housed the vixen and her cubs, a set far too large and deep to dig. I was surprised to find my organic cultivation farmer Cymaging the set to kill its occupants. That Sunday, my organic cultivator friend, who was a lay preacher with a sense of humour (a rare combination perhaps) gave a sermon concerning the real meaning of St Paul's 'There is a time.' My friends and I understood, even if the rest of the congregation failed to. Yet such attacks are fairly uncommon, and if poultry houses are kept locked at night and in a state of good repair, few thefts will take place.

There is little evidence, either, to support the popular opinion that foxes are sheep killers. Most Lakeland hunters are adamant that foxes do take lambs, but the statement is somewhat doubtful to say the least. Few foxes would face the rush of a Lakeland ewe defending her lamb, a rush that would put even the bravest dog to flight. Dead lambs, of course, are eaten, and skins are often found in the midden piles at the mouths of earths. These skins are, however, invariably from unburied lambs which have died of natural causes. Likewise, dead piglets may be found in these piles, though foxes never seem to be accused of pig killing. It seems likely that bad management of flocks, not foxes, is responsible for the death of lambs. But there are Lakeland farmers who genuinely do believe that foxes kill lambs. John Peel, the renowned fox-hunter of the Lakelands, recorded that he had once killed 'a notorious sheep-killing fox'.

Thus you have taken your first fox and killed it, justifying its death, perhaps, by the fact that foxes are considered vermin. To get a terrier really wed to fox, however, requires far more than merely one encounter with his foe. (Incidentally, few dog dealers will give a dog more than one joust prior to sale, for few can afford the time to train a dog to many foxes before selling.) Dogs really improve when given regular work, for not only do they get to know the ways of foxes, but the link between man and dog becomes very much stronger if the dog is worked regularly. The classic example of this is a bitch I bred called Climber, who became the property of Malcolm Haddock, the terrier man for the Meynell Hunt. Climber was worked so regularly that Haddock claimed that he could communicate to the bitch as to whether he wanted her to bolt or bottle up the fox prior to digging.

To my eternal shame, I had failed with this bitch and given her to Haddock because I failed to break her from stock worrying, let alone learnt to communicate with her. To those who disbelieve tales of such relationships, let me assure them that, if a person keeps and trains a dog regularly, links like these are readily formed. However, the buyer and seller, the dealer, the flash-in-the-pan terrier owner who will trade his dog for racing pigeons as one craze after another attracts him, will develop no such relationships, and will experience very little success with any livestock for that matter.

Many dogs who are worked regularly to fox learn to bolt them by dint of barking and without ever experiencing more than a scratch or so for their troubles. I once owned a bitch called Ping, a grand-daughter of John Cobby's old dog Pickaxe, and though she worked fox for ten or more years, she received one nip from a fox early in her career and never forgot it. For ever after she kept her distance, baying at the fox without tackling it. Contrariwise, however, many dogs become far too hard after a time at fox, and go all out to kill their foe after a fierce tussle. Certain terriers become very adroit at slaying foxes, particularly terriers which have bull terrier or Lakeland blood. Fell terriers characteristically slay foxes by throttling them to death, by seizing the fox with a throat-catch hold and twisting the muscle and fur of the throat until the creature is dead. Winch is fairly con-vinced that this is an inbred disposition in some Fell strains, but while it is not seen as a fault in the North, where foxes are considered to be vermin and hunts are staged to kill foxes rather than provide a spec-tacle, in the South it is thought of as a grievous fault, for terriers must provide sport for the field and a dead fox or a badly damaged fox limping from an earth is simply what is not required.

Once a terrier learns to kill a fox below ground, however, there is little its owner can do to remedy the fault for the dog becomes more dextrous at the task every time he goes to ground. All sorts of cures have been put forward by terrier men, ranging from allowing the dog to bay at a fox through a grid, or allowing the dog to work badger for a season. But, to be starkly frank, in a majority of cases these methods simply don't work. Once a dog has learned to fence for a throat hold, to come to grips and strangle his fox, there is little that can be done to prevent him doing it, and, as I have said, if he is given regular work, he will go on becoming ever more dextrous at slaying fox. I once had a rough-coated terrier bred by G. Hardwick of Blaengarw who was an ace at slaying foxes, though he was quite useless for work-ing with hounds. He would enter the earth with great care, take time assessing the position of his opponent and then get down to the task in deadly earnest. At no time would he bark or growl to give any

indication of his whereabouts. He was one of the best fox exterminators I have ever known, and one of the most useless hunt terriers I
have ever come across in the Midlands. His mute fury eventually
became his undoing when he was slain by a badger.

A dog should be capable of giving tongue, of course, for if one has
to dig to a terrier it is the only sure way to determine the position of
dog and fox. Mute dogs are fairly useless if one has to dig foxes, as
are dogs with weak, piping, falsetto squeaks. Dogs with a great deal
of bull terrier blood are usually guilty of being mute. John Russell
was said to dislike smooth-coated dogs for this reason (smooth-coated
fox terriers usually had a great deal of bull terrier blood at the time
when Russell was reputed to express this dislike of them). Furthermore, the mute dog is in great danger of being trapped below ground.
Joan Begbie, owner of the famous Seale Cottage strain of Jack Russell
terrier, once told me that she believed muteness was an inherited
factor in dogs. There does, though, seem to be an indication that it
is a fault which can be acquired during the process of entering. It is,
of course, a fault which it is nearly impossible to remedy.

Many foxes will play cat and mouse in a large earth, moving from
spot to spot when harassed by a terrier. Therefore block any exits,
but take care about this blocking, for foxes can squeeze through tiny
gaps and escape from seemingly impossibly small rabbit bolt-holes.
The blocking completed, wait awhile. Below your feet the barking
has settled to a steady staccato bay. Chances are your dog has
cornered his fox and is now facing him, a few feet or maybe only a
few inches away, giving tongue, shouting abuses, maybe chancing
a nip or two. If the unskilled puppy chances a bite or two, he will
usually learn the error of his ways, for the fox will retaliate and deliver
a series of short, sharp, stinging snaps, most of which will connect
on the terrier's face.

Listen carefully, for the sounds will tell you a lot about the battle
taking place a few feet below you. The staccato bay means that your
dog has cornered his foe, the roaring shriek that he is attacking the
fox, the high-pitched scream that he has not had things all his own
way and the fox has put in a few bites. There are men who boast they
can tell if the foe is a fox or badger simply by the sound of the baying.
I envy such skill, for I certainly don't have it.

The time has come to dig to your fox – so dig, and try to combine
speed and caution as you delve towards the sound of the fracas.
Caution is the operative word, for a puppy buried while at work will
often become a little reluctant to tackle his next fox, becoming what
is known as 'spade shy', coming off the fox as soon as the sound of
digging gets near for fear of being buried.

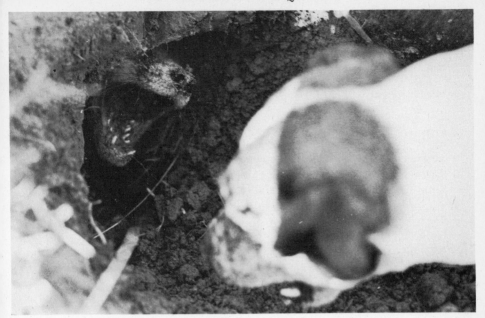

The end of a fox dig.

A fox drawn alive and unharmed.

Frankly, a great many various qualities must come together and jell before a terrier turns into a first-class fox-hunting terrier. Practice, however, certainly makes a dog, if not perfect, at least more proficient at the exacting task of fox digging.

Before the would-be terrier man bleats that he has no foxes on which he can try his terriers, let him examine any rubbish dump near a town. It is a racing certainty that there will be fox earths not a mile or so distant from these tips and rubbish dumps. The rubbish pile at Bentley, Walsall, while receiving regular bad publicity in the local newspaper for being what one councillor described as a major health hazard, is, I confess, a positive delight to hunt, for not only is it alive with rats, a quality that attracts hosts of the lads from the school where I teach, complete with ferrets and terriers, but it is also a haven for foxes. They are foxes in poor condition, admittedly, but foxes nevertheless. I feel decidedly hypocritical about chastizing my lads for playing truant to hunt this particular tip, for, if I told the truth, given half a chance, I would probably join them. Such is the 'do as I tell you, not as I do' world of the teacher, but, again, I digress.

Most of these earths are fairly shallow, and though many lie under bulky, immovable piles of refuse – huge slabs of damaged portions of the motorway which resemble urban versions of the legendary Lakeland borrans, and which are frankly equally dangerous – they still hold large numbers of foxes. Usually the earths are in large rabbit warrens and are dug out from the gritty, ashy, clinker-like soil. One such clinker pile has an enormously high percentage of sulphuric acid in its content, yet still was found to hold a litter of fox cubs. Earths on rubbish dumps are usually havens for mange mites, so care should be exercised when working a terrier in them. Even so, most are easy to dig, and it is not usually difficult to get permission to dig foxes on these dumps. Few authorities actually prosecute anyone for trespass on them, though a few prosecutions have been known, I must admit. Oddly enough, itinerants who seek scrap on the tips will pass unnoticed by the authorities, but hunters with terriers and ferrets may well be viewed with suspicion unless they have got permission first. It is a bit pointless trying to poach foxes anyway, since how do you, if challenged, conceal or explain away a four-feet-deep hole?

Not all fox earths are quite so easy to dig, of course, and some are positive death traps for terriers. Two earths near Consett, County Durham, are renowned for claiming the lives of terriers. Such earths are not only often very deep, but some are also enlarged tracts in the subterranean rocks, produced by several million years of weathering. Many have faults and hidden crevices, totally undetectable in the blackness of the set, where a dog can plummet down several feet.

Only the smart-Alec, conceited fool will attempt to work such earths after terrier men have warned him of their reputation, but, year in, year out, notorious earths still claim the lives of terriers. Pit workings or earths near drift mines are legendary death traps. Not only are the rocks there crumbly and rotten, the roofs of the drifts unsafe, but also pockets of suffocating methane and hydrogen sulphide can kill any unwary dog who, maddened by its proximity to fox, ventures into the gas pockets and is soon panting for breath. I know of one such earth near my birthplace in Wales. It is a drift mine which has caused the deaths of hundreds of terriers. Yet each new generation of terrier men yields up fresh victims for these earths. The borrans, or rocky earths of the North have very unsavoury reputations for being death to terriers.

Even the most innocuous-looking earths can be death traps and a great deal deeper than they appear. One such example springs instantly to mind. I had been staying with the McLeods in the Grampians, for old John was not only a font of wisdom concerning Highland wildlife and folk legend, but also an excellent terrier man, a little past digging when I knew him, but he knew every inch of the land that he, his father and grandfather had keepered. One of his sons had bought a greyhound dog, a big black, retired track dog, a son of Hi There, so far as I remember, and was keen to try it on fox. Old John asked if one of my bitches was absolutely sound on fox, and on being assured she was, we walked up the hill towards a one-eyed set almost covered in deep heather, only noticeable because of the well-used track which led through the heather to the earth. I was surprised to find the boys – heck, boys, they're nearly forty now – going along the floor of the valley nearly three quarters of a mile away and stationing the greyhound near a wind-blasted hawthorn bush. I put in Clown, a prick-eared, ugly but useful bitch, and heard her pad her way into the blackness. Silence, and not even a faint yicker to indicate that she had found. 'She's not at home, John,' I muttered, and bent down to call the bitch out, but John pushed his thumb stick across my throat, for he is a man with laconic manners, and pointed to a spot close to where his boys were. A minute or so later, a small vixen flashed out of the rocks near the lads and was nailed rather raggedly by the greyhound after a course of only twenty yards. Clown followed her out. This was *not* a one-eyed set. McLeod assured me that story had it that foxes had been in this earth before the wolves had left Glencoe. A deep set is not necessarily always characterized by a great number of entrances and exits.

Large numbers of dogs inevitably come to grief in such sets, and there is little one can do to prevent it, apart from listening to the advice of men who have already had bad experiences. There is an earth on a canal bank near Wall, in Staffordshire, originally an old Roman fortress, that I've seen acting like a magnet to terrier men ever since I've been in the area. There are always foxes at home in this earth even after a wet spell in mid-summer, but the place is thwart with danger. Scarcely a terrier man in the district does not regret having encountered the place, and the number of terriers' lives it has claimed must be staggering. The earth starts out as an innocent, one-holed set, and goes deep into rotted sandstone, emerging ninety feet down the canal bank. I know it well, for the bones of two of my terriers are down there somewhere, for I too failed, or refused, to heed the advice given to me by Joe Wadlow who once did some earth stopping for the South Staffordshire Hunt during the First World War.

The Fell and Moorland Club offers an excellent rescue service, even hiring excavating equipment to delve to find lost dogs. They have a fair degree of success, but, sadly, an even greater number of failures, for to dig to a trapped dog is one thing, to resuscitate a suffocated corpse quite another. Even so, the Fell and Moorland offer excellent insurance against massive excavation fees and certainly help to rescue many dogs otherwise doomed to certain death in apparently undiggable earths. The rescues published in the Club's *Year Books* read like epics and give vivid descriptions of the problems involved in rescuing dogs from impossible earths. Membership is an excellent investment for any terrier man, since it costs less than a pound a year to belong to this estimable club.

Now for a slight digression. I expect a very high standard of obedience from my dogs, for I insist that they should come out of an earth when called. Since the publication of *The Working Terrier*, I have found myself under a fair amount of attack on this point. Many hunters seem to prefer having a dog that will stick to its foe the fox through thick and thin, regardless of the cries of their owners calling the terrier off. I, for one, would not wish this to be so. When I've had enough of a dig, and I must confess I quit very difficult earths, for I am fond of hunting alone, I want a dog out and on its way regardless of what anyone says about quitting. Still, if it's a dog who will stay regardless of command, well, yours the time, yours the dog. Sufficient to say, I have spent four days digging for a friend's dog only to find the animal was not trapped, merely disobedient and unbroken to rabbit. For my money, I would have hated to have owned such a terrier, yet have to confess that in my early days I did own dogs like that.

Foxes rarely, if ever, stay living below ground all the year round.

Summer sees them away from the fetid, mange-ridden earth, taking cover in kale and corn, sheltering under hedges during rain storms. In late autumn, they return to the earths, and the approach of winter is usually the best time to find foxes below ground. In late winter, the vixen and dog pair and the cubs are born fifty-six days or so after the fertilization of the ova – the actual gestation period is again a matter for debate according to recent scientific articles. Fox cubs are born blue-black to chocolate brown, and also thickly furred, for foxes, unlike badgers, do not draw bedding, so good insulation is needed if the cub is not to die from hypothermia. Whether or not the dog fox assists in rearing the cubs is somewhat open to question. Personally I am highly sceptical as to whether he gives much assistance at all. He certainly stays fairly closely at hand during the rearing of the cubs, possibly out of curiosity, possibly because of some emotional attachment to the vixen – an attachment that persists after he has served her. It is a fair to moderate certainty that, where a hunter finds a vixen with a litter of cubs, a few hundred yards away will be an earth which houses the dog fox.

At Ewden, just north of Rotherham, I once found two vixens had dug breeding earths only twenty yards from each other, while another hundred yards away I found the earth of a dog fox. It seems just a little likely that foxes are sometimes polygamous. The male certainly guards territory with great ferocity against rival males. Indeed, Robert Ardrey believes that battles between creatures of the same species are largely territorial, battles to secure mates being rarely, if ever, fought. For a period of about three years, the area around my cottage was patrolled by a big rangy dog fox, and I saw very few other male foxes in the district. When at last the old dog fox expired, young males swarmed into the district, dividing up the territory like gipsy heirs.

But now we may assume that your dog is entered to fox. Let's therefore examine a few alternative methods of taking our quarry. First, all earths can be blocked, and, if the terrier gives tongue well, it is reasonably easy, provided the earth is not too deep, to dig to such a dog. Most foxes, given a chance, will bolt rather than fight, however, for foxes simply don't want confrontations and savage battles with dogs. In practice, foxes have a pronounced fear of dogs, and even vixens with cubs will bolt and desert their cubs given half a chance. Story-book tales of foxes battling against hordes of terriers to protect their cubs are a bit suspect, to say the least. So the fox bolts. How, then, might he be taken?

If one is quiet and has a useful terrier, the sort inclined to bark and bolt the fox rather than thrash it to death, foxes can be taken by netting them with large, strongly made purse nets. Foxes quite often bolt to ferrets when they have holed up in a rabbit earth, and I know several ferreters who have actually taken foxes in their rabbit nets. Once a fox hits the nets, however, be sharp about unravelling him, particularly if he is tangled in a rabbit net by accident. Most foxes, on finding themselves trapped in the net, simply go into a state near to catalepsy. Many hunters consider that the fox is simply playing possum, or acting dead to escape the attention of the hunter and his dog. This is untrue. The unconsciousness, the state of near catalepsy, is quite simply a fit – as genuine and unfeigned as the fits of Silas Marner. Beware, however, should you seek to unravel your still-live quarry. Such fits are quickly induced, and recovery is equally rapid. The hunter will suddenly find he has a raging, snapping, spitting fiend in his hands. Live foxes should be gripped with both hands, one hand around the neck, one around the loin.

Having given this excellent advice, may I confess yet once again to being something of a hypocrite about it. I have an inch-long scar on my left forearm as a result of handling a live fox that came out of its state of catalepsy very quickly. If I have a failing, and a bad failing, it is that I continue to lecture long after school is over. I had bolted and netted a fox for some female photographers, one of whom treacherously gave the photographs to an anti-bloodsports organization – photographs which showed the fox with his teeth embedded in my arm. This happened just as I was in the process of lecturing on my theory of catalepsy and holding the fox. My attention was distracted by a flash bulb going off, and the terrified vixen came to life instantly and bit straight through my arm, locking like a bulldog and setting in to await the inevitable with eyes glazed and jaws tightening by the second. I had one hell of a time persuading her to let go. I have an incredible collection of sporting photographs, but there is one I simply don't show to anyone but my very close friends: the one which depicts me hopping around, fox fixed to my arm and my face registering such panic as to convince anyone of my utter inability to handle a live fox.

Coursing bolted foxes with greyhounds or lurchers is a most efficient way of catching them, far more efficient than hunting fox with hounds. It is perhaps equally spectacular, but certainly not such a social event. Nevertheless, it is certainly more efficient, as I have said. Last year the Meynell Hunt had a moderate haul of foxes – the cost of taking such a haul being above £20,000, or so I have been told. Ten miles from the hunt kennel lives a noted fox poacher who killed nearly twice as many foxes using a mongrelly Jack Russell terrier bitch and a ragged-looking lurcher dog. People who tell you that fox

A tremendous day's hunting using terriers and a lurcher.

hunts are efficient ways of controlling foxes are fooling you and themselves. I simply wish they would own up to the fact that fox hunting
is a social event, not a vendetta between hunt followers and foxes.
Perhaps, if they told the truth, the League Against Cruel Sports
would not make itself as difficult and annoying on hunt days. Fox
hunting with hounds and horses in hunt regalia simply isn't intended
to be efficient. It represents merely an interesting day out. At all
events, I have dealt fully with the welding of lurcher and terrier into
a fox-hunting team in *The Working Terrier*, and would refer the interested reader to that book.

During the last two years of the 1970s, there was a boom in
fox-pelt prices. Ten years earlier, you couldn't give them away, or,
rather, sell them for more than £4. At the time of writing, they fetch
around £20. In ten years' time, they may be worth next to nothing
again. Such is the fickle market in pelts. Of course, in any case, no
furrier is interested in a badly damaged pelt from a fox that has been
baited to death or ragged after death. Therefore dispatch the fox
quickly, with the minimum amount of pain, if you intend to profit
from the pelt. Skin your fox as soon as it is dead. If the hunter waits

71

until the carcass is cool, it becomes a far more difficult task, for the skin on freshly killed foxes practically slides off the body. Skin by cutting from vent to hind legs and sleeve the skin as one would do a rabbit. Next cut up the belly of the fur with a sharp knife, and nail the skin, stretching it tightly to a wooden frame – an old door will do – skin side outwards, fur side inwards. Scrape off all fat, as this attracts flies as soon as the weather warms up and a fly-blown pelt is worth next to nothing.

It pays to examine a pelt and to know why furriers pay as much or as little for fox skins as they do. Blue marks on the skin side of the pelt indicate moult was taking place and the fur will usually slip out from such areas once the pelt is cured. Such a pelt is worth little as it can only be used to trim fur for fur collars or to patch fur on the teenage fun-fur coats. Prime pelts are, in fact, quite rare, and even domesticated foxes only hold prime pelts for a matter of weeks. Also remember that the prices which furriers offer to pay in their advertisements for pelts is the maximum price they intend to pay. Poor-grade pelts obviously fetch less. Curing skins is fairly easy, or so I've been told. I've never been able to make a good job of it, unfortunately, and my pelts usually finish up as stiff as boards, unlike those of my close friend, Moses Smith, who is quite expert at curing. There are, of course, firms who specialize in curing good pelts. Chapmans of Tutbury is one, and these firms invariably make an excellent job of them. For those who would like to try pelt curing at home, though, may I refer them to *Tan Your Hide* by Phyllis Hobson, an excellent book which gives details on several methods of curing pelts. May I also wish the home pelt curer the very best of luck. I have been singularly unsuccessful at curing skins.

Before leaving the subject of fox catching with terriers, it should be emphasized that foxes are carrion eaters, gorging on filth that would sicken a dog, and oddly enough thriving on such mess. Old carcasses, remains of birds and rodents that litter the breeding earths and midden piles left by foxes are usually fairly pungent. It is not therefore surprising that bites received from foxes invariably go bad. If a hunter is bitten by a fox, he will be very wise to consult a doctor. I have been through the stages of home physician-cum-backwoodsman when I was damn fool enough to reject the principles of modern medical science in favour of herbal cures. I can assure the reader that most homespun remedies for curing the effects of fox bites, such as pouring whisky into the wound or cauterizing with a red-hot cobblers' awl (I cringe at the thought), are usually fairly useless. Against the advice of Moses, whose wisdom concerning the treatment of maladies such as wounds, running sores and so forth puts me to shame, I

Fox bites invariably cause massive facial swellings.

treated a bad fox bite I received while separating a fox from a tussle with a terrier. I must have used all the remedies suggested by Lucas, Cobby, and even Jorrocks, and within days my arm had swollen to the size of a marrow and, horror of horrors, bright red lines began to creep from the wound to my shoulder. Finally I stopped playing at Daniel Boone and did the sensible thing – went to the doctor. After a huge dose of antibiotics, a sermon about lunacy and threats of committal notices from my physician who was also, thank heavens, a close friend, my arm resumed normal size, though it was extremely painful for weeks after the wound had apparently healed.

Incidentally, rat bites are far more dangerous than even fox bites. Likewise, dogs that have been bitten by foxes are also likely to become very badly infected unless the wounds are cleaned and cleaned well. A mild antiseptic is useful, but at the first sign of persistent swelling or the slightest sign of sepsis, a vet should be consulted. The faces of dogs bitten by foxes invariably swell up like pumpkins, but after a day or so these swellings should subside. If they don't, never play at physician yourself, or worse still at God. Get the dog to a vet straight away.

The Badger

Next on the list of quarry comes the badger, and a formidable beast he is. I am prepared to gamble that if a terrier owner simply mentions that he owns Jack Russell terriers to some ageing countryman – one without dogs at the moment, probably – that self-same countryman will tell the tiro man how years ago he owned a dog which actually killed a badger. What an incredible animal that terrier would be, but what an incredible liar the raconteur. Like Keith Waterhouse's Billy Liar, I often question if there ever were any wise old men. Quite simply, the badger is the age-old archetypal grappler, the foe *par excellence*, the doyen of fighting beasts, the greatest pound-for-pound battler the Almighty has yet produced. He is also damn nigh invulnerable to the attack of a 14-pound terrier. Believe me, a dog that attempts to try and polish off a badger is, as they say in the Black Country, on to a 'hiding to nothing'. Two stories should help to convince the reader of the truth of this statement.

In 1800, give or take a decade or so, the North of England succeeded in producing a hell of a good fighting dog called the Blue Paul. Some authorities say that this was a hybrid 'twixt terrier and bulldog, others state that it was a mixture of mastiff and bulldog; but, whatever it was, it was an outstanding fighting dog and weighed in at a minimum of 60 pounds, with some specimens reaching almost 100 pounds – the sort of dog that can put a lion to flight, though that's not entirely true, since several were reputedly killed by lions in the Cape. At the time of the breed's popularity, the pubs of London began to organize a seedy type of contest between dogs and badgers, sometimes backing the dog to draw the badger from the barrel, sometimes pitting the dog actually to kill the wild beast. It was a seemingly very uneven contest: a ferocious fighting dog weighing up to 100 pounds against a pitiful Kenneth Grahame type of beast – that is, until one saw the records of such fights. Even the Blue Paul was bested by this creature – a creature that rarely scaled in at 40 pounds, even in winter fat.

Thus, if a dog of the calibre of this beast came off badly, a Jack Russell terrier is certainly not going to be victor of any dog *versus* Brock battle. Some time ago, a bull terrier breeder went to Crufts with a dog that had reputedly killed a badger, and was surrounded by hosts of admiring townies who believed his story. Town dwellers overrate dogs, and probably have never seen a badger anyway. As they chatted, I stroked the dog, examining the underside of the jaw and the neck – places where badgers always inflict damage. The dog was unmarked. It is doubtful whether either dog or man had ever

74

seen a badger, let alone dug and tackled one. Any dog that has tried to slug it out with a badger will bear the unmistakable marks of the combat.

The second tale is even more telling of the badger's fighting ability. Immediately prior to a fox hunt with hounds – usually the night before the hunt – the hunt terrier man is required to block all difficult earths to prevent the fox running a field or so and going to ground as soon as he is pressed. A bit unsporting, if one considers John Masefield's poem *Reynard the Fox*, a poem that made most of my school friends very critical of fox hunting indeed. The fact is, however, that very many foxes simply run a field and go to ground – sensible, but not conducive to an exciting hunt for the field. Well, our local terrier man is extremely thorough and efficient and had blocked a very deep badger earth with stakes and heavy stones. No fox could get to ground there, and even a badger would have had a heck of a time shifting the heavy rocks to dig his way out. Most terrier men unblock the earths immediately after the hunt anyway. Subsequently, the terrier man not only blocked out the foxes, but also a fiery old boar badger who was out foraging when the earth stopping was being done. Next day the hounds drew a cover near the set and all hell broke loose literally. The boar was lifted, shaken and thrown by the hounds, who yelled and screamed at the effects of the combat while the huntsmen furiously tried to break up the mêlée. After a battle that must have lasted a full quarter of an hour, the badger shuffled away with his rolling, bear-like gait so characteristic of badgers. The hounds were frightfully mauled, but the badger, though bruised, seemed quite intact and unhurt. Many hound packs do, it is true, break up badgers, but the damage inflicted by an adult boar on hounds is devastating. Alison Craig of Oregon, a keen hunter, assures me that she has seen a cougar back down to the American badger, a related and similar species, and that ratels, an aggressive, more dynamic African version of poor old Brock, have actually attacked fully grown black buffalo when they are enraged. Terriers simply don't stand a chance against such creatures.

Why, then, is the badger so invulnerable? In addition to being a stoat, one of the most ferocious little fighters known to man, the badger has added advantage over his mustelid cousins. The hide of the badger is very tough: so tough that skinning and curing presents something of a problem for all but a professional skin curer. Furthermore, below the hide is a layer of pungent fat, a fat that becomes a semi-fluid-like oil when it is warm. Furthermore, the beast's jaws are quite unique, for they are hinged into the skull. Therefore the jaws just do not dislocate like the jaws of other mammals when under

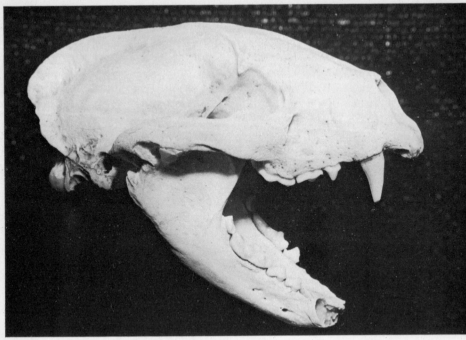

A badger skull is hinged and it is nearly impossible for the jaw to dislocate.

stress. They break sometimes, rarely would be more accurate, but cannot dislocate without extensive damage to the very thick skull of the badger. Furthermore, badger bones are extremely dense and therefore really hard to damage (see the accompanying photograph of the skull of this beast). Couple these defensive mechanisms with the fact that the beast has a bite like a steel trap and claws (usually used for digging) nearly an inch and a half long, and you have a fair assessment of your foe, and, believe me, a foe he really is. I repeat: no dog can kill a badger. Badgers have lived in Britain since the Ice Age, and, although savagely persecuted, there is little doubt that they are still far from uncommon, far from being the endangered species which some naturalists tell us they are. To survive such treatment as has been dealt out by the British sportsman (tongue in cheek to write that word in this context) they have to be tough. Again, I have dealt with this quarry very thoroughly in *The Working Terrier*, so it is expedient merely to touch on the subject now.

As I have said, badgers are far from rare. They are perhaps the most adaptable of stoats and also the slowest, though, after watching a snared one strike at my terrified lurcher recently, slow is hardly the word I could use. They live on the most varied diet. Food samples taken from the stomach of trapped badger indicate that they eat considerable quantities of vegetable matter, far more than would a fox. Bread scraps are regularly salvaged from my dustbin by night-feeding badgers who live in the badger set behind my cottage, and the potato clamps in a neighbouring village are regularly opened up by a pair of scavengers. Bluebell bulbs are a passion with badgers. Insects also provide a large amount of animal protein – indigestible even to the digestive tracts of Brock, as the casings are found intact in the droppings. They are not impartial to really ripe carrion, either, and will regularly raid the midden piles of poultry farms. Rabbits are taken sometimes, though they would have to be crippled or diseased for a badger to catch one. Rabbit kittens often fall casualties to badgers, particularly when the rabbit nests in stops close to the surface. Some years ago, I was asked to rid some land of badgers as they were creating a nuisance by ripping the sides out of beehives – probably to get the eggs and larvae of the bees rather than to eat the honey. Maybe, however, they do have a penchant for honey as well, for many naturalists, including T. H. White, refer to them as the last British bear. Stoats they are, however, through and through, as you will certainly realize once you have decided to hunt them.

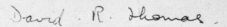

    I authorise Mr. Alun.S.Thomas to remove a

badger from my land, of which I am the owner.

    The above badger is a nuisance and I would like

it removed.

                David . R . Thomas .

A permit is required before a hunter is allowed to dig badger.

Before hunting the badger, however, we must take a quick look at the law concerning badger digging, and a lunatic law it is. Badgers are a semi-protected species (yet another tongue-in-cheek statement, reader, about a tongue-in-cheek subject). In 1973, the British government in its wisdom passed the highly controversial Badger Protection Act. It was, on first impression, an extremely harsh law, with fines of up to £200 for the taking of badger and a similar fine for the possession of fresh badger skins. But then, of course, when we come to examine what can only be called the small print of the contract, the Act states that it is illegal to take a badger unless one has permission from the landowner (in writing, of course, since bureaucracy always

insists on written permission), stating that the animal is causing a nuisance. I have always suspected that this Act was drawn up to satisfy the anti-field-sports contingent who, unknowing of the ways of badgers and badger diggers, did not realize that a badger dig can last for hours, and sometimes days, the dig itself often growing to resemble an excavation job done by a major building contractor. It is fairly impossible to poach badger without detection, and almost every digger I know secures permission to dig badger before he begins his task. There have been, of course, several prosecutions of near-lunatics who were actually found trespassing in pursuit of badger, and quite recently there has been a revival in badger baiting which has given the sensational side of the press a field day. There has, however, been little by way of prosecution of unlawful badger diggers recently. 'The law is an ass, Mr Bumble,' as I believe Dickens wrote.

Perhaps the controversy has been clouded by investigations into the disease of cattle and man called brucellosis or contagious abortion. Researches have shown that badgers are carriers of the disease, and milk-farming areas, which incidentally are usually the habitats of badgers, have subsequently become most anti-badger indeed, the badger growing so unpopular that pest control officers simply pump Cymag down the sets, leaving Brock to die a rapid though agonizing death through hydrocyanic acid gas poisoning. I feel quite sorry for the badger. He must be totally baffled by man's contrary interest in him. The whole badger problem must seem like a medieval riddle: when is a protected creature not a protected creature? Answer: when it is a badger.

But the badger is our quarry, so how to take him. I have to confess it is a bit of a problem. First, it is advisable that any terrier which is now to enter to badger should have had considerable experience at fox before he meets the more formidable Brock underground. Make a quick assessment of the badger's defence mechanism when it is attacked by a terrier. As we have seen, a fox will bolt if it can, and only fight or dig in if it must. Badgers are a different kettle of fish. Provided it is on its home ground and not in a temporary refuge of a drain or an artificial earth, it is extremely unlikely that a badger will bolt. Therefore he must be dug, and a dog must be trained to bottle him up in one of the blind alleys of the set – a dog trained to bay like thunder to direct the delving of the diggers, and a dog, in fact, with a rare combination of qualities; but more of these later. First take a look at the lair of the badger, the seat, set or sette, call it what you will, spell it as you like. It is an amazing piece of design work.

A badger set that is obviously in use. Note the striations caused by the badger's claws.

Badgers are habitual diggers. The very word badger is derived from the French verb *becher* – 'to dig', and dig he must, for just as the hawk with his wings clipped will fret and pine, so a badger denied the right to dig will become a pitiful mental wreck in no time at all. Those who have reared badgers, and, to my eternal discredit, I am among them, will confirm that they make unsatisfactory pets for not only are they extremely musky, utterly destructive in their ways, but their desire to mine makes them totally unsuitable as house animals. Mine actually took up quarry tiles and wore its huge claws to the quick trying to burrow into the cement. Even as zoo creatures they are unsatisfactory, for they are nocturnal and rarely come to the surface by day, preferring to tunnel beneath existing tunnels, and then, when those have fallen in, to tunnel into the ruins of their citadels.

Some badger sets are enormous. One in Hinckley was old before Napoleon began his campaigns and produced fighting boars second to none – boars fit to delight the macabre interests of Regency England and to provide money aplenty for the diggers – hard-earned money mind you, for the set is enormous. In 1820, badgers from Leicester fetched as much as £5 apiece in the bloody pits of London, pits which, as folk legend has it, resounded with the screams of stricken beasts long after the 1835 Act ostensibly stopped the barbarism. Sets sixty feet deep are not all that uncommon in places where rotted sandstone or oolitic limestone constitutes the substrata. Many are so deep that electronic locating devices (bleepers) fitted to dogs stop giving any reading. Others are so vast, and filled with pockets of foul air – air to which the badger is amazingly tolerant, incidentally – that dogs without number have vanished into their depths, sunk without trace, as the saying goes. Furthermore, sets drilled through solid rock, the work of countless generations of badgers, present hazards to terrify the would-be terrier man about to enter his dog to badger.

My own local badger set is quite famous. At one time the South Staffordshire Hunt dreaded it, and since the owners – who are, incidentally, passionate badger conservationists – refuse to allow earth stopping, any fox in the neighbourhood hightailed it for the set whenever danger threatened. About ten years since, give or take a year, I entered a terrier into this earth, a terrier broken to badger, as there were foxes using the lairs and the owner of the land wanted to be rid of Reynard but the badgers left alone. My dog was to ground six hours, and bolted five foxes from the holes, five hundred yards apart in some cases. Such a citadel is often centuries old, filled with pitfalls and hazards and frankly best given a miss.

A 'scratch' tree – a sure sign an established badger colony is nearby.

In the Fells, badgers sometimes fail to dig their own sets but simply dwell among the glacial boulders, though how their digging urges are sublimated in these rocky conditions is rather baffling. These earths are, of course, impossible to dig, as many of the boulders carried by the ice to their final resting places are several tons in weight. Even so, there are terrier men fool enough to enter a dog even here. Of course, the place is a death trap, and while a pathetic cub or so may be carried out by a terrier once in a while, it is unlikely that anyone could even do any real badger digging in such places. Nigel Hinch-cliffe, Chairman of the Pennine Fox Hounds, a pack that had to run in some of the most difficult country in Britain, tells of one earth, the opening of which is a slide of forty feet down smooth slippery rock. It is possible to bolt fox from such places as this now and again, but, once a badger is established in a set like this, only disease, famine or poison will cause him to leave.

In the Shires, most badger sets start as the result of a male or female leaving the set and excavating a warren to catch a rabbit. Now, badgers dig at a heck of a pace – a foot a minute in sandy soil, Cobby estimated – and in no time at all Brock has forgotten his rabbit and is enlarging his new set. Sets like these are remarkably easy to dig. Some years ago, Gerry Humphries and I dug out a young male which had enlarged such a rabbit earth and was lying up in a short stop four feet long and a foot below the surface. But while it was a remarkably easy dig, it is extremely rare to find a badger in such a dangerously vulnerable place. Artificial earths, designed by hunts-men as spots where foxes might rear cubs in peace, often harbour solitary boars – boars that have lost a territorial battle with their sires and have been driven off from the main set. Capel put down many of these earths, and badgers were a great nuisance since they hogged the drains, refusing the foxes a chance to breed. Some hunts do encourage badgers, though, as once earths in a given area become cursed with mange mites (*Sarcoptes communis*), a badger will (or, is supposed to, would be more accurate) clean the earth by digging out the mange-ridden soil. Personally, I believe this to be a fallacy, but it was an idea very prevalent during the golden age of fox hunting when badgers were tolerated because of the notion.

Having dealt with the earths and the nature of the quarry, we come to a very controversial subject: namely, the closed season for the hunting of badger. Legally, of course, there is no closed season and no doubt if the government were to enforce such a closed season it could be expected to be yet another extremely ill-advised regulation. As things stand, it is up to the terrier man to ensure that badger are not hunted during the breeding season. It is believed that badgers

The almost legendary Brough's Earths – probably the largest badger set in the world. Over the centuries over a thousand tons of earth have been excavated by badgers.

A deceptive 'one eye' set. This earth has been the burial ground of many terriers.

couple some time in late summer, but no one is actually certain of the gestation period of Brock, the cubs being born in or about February. It is therefore madness to slip a terrier into an earth where cubs are likely to be found, for whereas the sire and dam of the babes are invulnerable, the cubs are certainly not. Furthermore, contrary to the story-book tales usually written by those ill-versed in the ways of badgers, and who have probably never even seen one, few sows actively defend their young, preferring to slink off into the set, perhaps to draw the fire of the dog. It rarely works, for the terriers find newly born cubs easy meat and create mayhem among them. Not only is this a bit barbarous, or, to say the least, unsporting, but it has a decidedly bad effect on future hunting.

Every hunter worthy of the name hunter, not butcher, should give a care for the future of the species he is hunting. If he doesn't do so, but slaughters beasts indiscriminately, then the badger will go the way of the dodo, the great auk and the British wolf. The badger population of Cardiganshire is taking a tremendous beating as a result of indiscriminate slaughter of cubs and adults at the very time of writing. Since the cubs are born early in the year, the digger would do well to confine his activities to the summer months.

Now for entering and digging. First, most seasoned hunters prefer to work dogs to fox for a season before trying them to badger. Badger is a dangerous quarry, so the hunter will be well advised to get his terrier experienced in the pursuit of lesser game below ground before tackling the heavy stuff. Many hunters test their terriers to badger before the dogs have ever even seen a fox, and the reasons are obvious. Foxes are itinerant and the hunter will often walk miles and experience many fruitless hunts before he meets up with a fox that is to ground. Badgers are not itinerant, however, and are always at home to callers. Thus they are easy to find. Sadly, or perhaps fortunately, they are not so easy to take. Still, if the terrier man can work his dogs to fox for a season before trying Brock, so much the better.

Normally a dog will enter to badger fairly easily if it has worked fox for a season or so, and I have in fact known some dogs that are mad keen to tackle badger, even though they refuse to look at a fox. It should be pointed out that the reverse can also be so, for Climber, the bitch mentioned earlier, was a superb bitch to fox but turned into an inveterate coward when faced with even a half-grown badger cub. Gaston Phoebus, a famous hunter of the Middle Ages, describes a singularly barbarous method of entering a sapling terrier to badger. A boar badger was caught and the lower jaw severed by means of large metal cutters. The terriers were then tried at the near-harmless, pitiful creature, who, without a lower jaw, was unable to punish the

A delving rod is a priceless tool to ascertain the depth of an earth.

Trenching through to the sound of the baying: the start of a badger dig.

terrier. This staggering method of entering is as incongruous as it is revolting. To begin with, I am doubtful as to whether a badger could survive after its jaws were severed, and secondly, such a method would teach a terrier a set of false, and dangerously false, values. Might not a puppy taught by this method have thrown all caution to the wind and launched himself at the first unmaimed badger he saw, believing it was unable to retaliate?

A first-rate badger dog should have four basic qualities. First, he should be brave, but not too brave; more like the little bear's porridge, in fact; in other words, 'just right'. Should he be really afraid of the badger, he may bark at the badger's bedding in the first empty sleeping compartment, a problem quite frequently encountered when hunting a slightly nervous terrier to badger; or else stay so far from the cornered badger that the beast manages to regain the main set again, thereby making all the digging fruitless. Should he be too brave and attempt a catch hold or tackle below ground, he will find out to his cost the power of the beast he is against.

A hard dog, the sort that refuses to give ground, will be very quickly *hors de combat* and in need of veterinary treatment. Some strains of Fell terrier are demons to fox, but absolutely useless against badger. Not through lack of courage, mind you, but quite the reverse, for they tend to wade in, chance a hold fearlessly, take a tremendous thrashing and become crippled, maimed and made old before their time, all because of a lack of discretion in handling such formidable quarry. Willie Irving, the greatest of the Fell hunters since Piper Allen, it has been said, regularly remarked that the Lakeland terrier (Willie was responsible for the Kennel Club acceptance and its standardizing) was of little use for badger hunting since it was quite simply too hard. Hence the ideal dog for this sport has to be 'just right', be prepared to spend its time baying and darting at the cornered badger, staying put in the Stygian blackness of the centre of the set, keeping his distance from the badger's jaws and heedless of the flying earth which the badger kicks up during the hunt; for badgers, true to their name, endeavour to bury themselves in the earth, to throw up a wall of earth 'twixt them and the dog when they are frightened.

Next the dog must have a good strong voice. Foolish as this sounds, it is one of the most important qualities. A mute dog is practically useless, and a dog with a weak, piping trill is nearly as bad. Badgers often stand to fight deep in the set, and to delve to them satisfactorily one must have a dog with a deep, resonant, *basso profundo* voice to guide the digger. I once dug a boar near Maltby, Yorkshire, that was down nearly fifteen feet, and found him only because of the thunder-

A badger is tailed at the end of a dig.

End of the dig — a badger's ursine head appears at the end of the excavation.

A badger, alive and unharmed, is crated and transported to a new home.

ous baying of a very useful bitch I owned at the time. Now I will have to finish the story, even if it does brand me as a crass amateur. We trenched through and eventually crowned in on top of the pair, the bitch screaming like an angry banshee. I reached down to draw the bitch, for it is lunacy to allow the dog to suffer the scrimmage which takes place when a badger is about to be tailed, and, as I drew her, in her excitement she struck at my hands. I lifted her clear of my body, rolled slightly to get her snapping jaws clear of my face and turned to see the badger shuffle off into the main set. I must admit I gave him best. It was late evening, raining, and my team of diggers was absolutely exhausted. No one spoke to me on the way home from that dig. But show me the hunter who has never made a mistake.

Furthermore, the dog should stay to his quarry for a good length of time. I've known dogs stay twenty hours to a badger, and only last year I dug a very old bitch who'd stayed twenty-nine hours. If a dog nips in and out every few minutes, the badger will quite simply

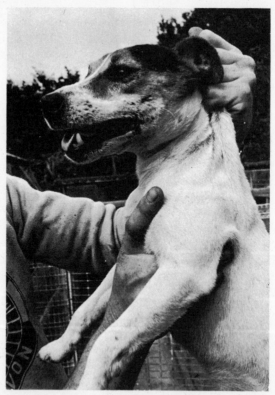

Badger bites are quite distinct from the wounds inflicted by foxes and are usually 'pincer-like' nips inflicted on the lower jaw and neck of the dog.

waddle off into the main set and the job will begin again. I rate nose highly in badger dogs. I have a bitch in my possession, geriatric now, I'm afraid, who could locate a badger that had dug in behind a wall of soil. Working a stop, for this is what badger diggers usually call the process, a dog has to have a very efficient nose to locate a badger behind this loose soil in a musk-filled set. A strong, powerful, dog is priceless at the end of the dig to fix or hold the badger. The best I ever saw was a huge, ugly, rough-haired dog owned by Bob Walker of Rugeley. This dog wouldn't go to ground, he was too big anyway, but 'when the kissing had to stop' and the rough and tumble at the end of the dig occurred, he was priceless. As with most Caesar dogs, as this kind of dog is called, he came to a sticky end, however. Sadly, this is an occupational hazard with Caesar dogs who have to bear the brunt of the battle at the end of the dig.

I must confess I dislike killing badgers. I once, as I said, reared one as a pet, and though he proved one heck of a nuisance, it certainly taught me to like Brock rather than harm him.

The Otter

The badger is certainly one of the most dangerous beasts the terrier is likely to encounter, but so also is the otter. Since I wrote *The Working Terrier*, the otter has become a protected beast in Britain, though he is still hunted north of the border. Like the badger, he is also a stoat, an elegant, fast-biting, aquadynamic beast who will give a good account of himself against a 60-pound hound, let alone a 14-pound terrier. As a pound-for-pound battler, the otter certainly takes some beating. Before the reader sets off for Scotland to pit his terrier against this aquatic fitch, may I suggest he reads Henry Williamson's *Tarka the Otter* and dwells for a while on the final battle between the drafted stag hound, Deadlock, a huge ponderous beast, a relic of Norman times, and the darting, quicksilver Tarka. The battle which finishes with the death of both (the screen version is a joy to watch, a masterpiece of authenticity, enough to delight even the critical, ascetic Williamson), gives some indication of the fighting power of the otter.

Lucas hunted otter with his team of Sealyhams, real Sealyhams, not the heavy cumbersome beasts of today, and his book *The Sealyham Terrier* is as interesting as his more commonly known *Hunt and Working Terriers*. An otter can give any terrier team a heck of a bad time, and much of the fighting will take place in deep water in conditions where the terrier man will have little control over the outcome of the contest. Alys Serrell, whose book *With Hound and Terrier in the Field* is a far more interesting and well-written book than its rather heavy-going title suggests, hunted otter with her team of fox terriers – again, real fox terriers, unspoilt by the world of show breeders. Russell-type terriers will still give a good performance against these beasts. The northern hunter Piper Allen – a famous otter hunter and a worker of the common stock of dog that spawned both the Bedlington and the Dandie Dinmont – worked his puppies to water rats along the brooks and streams before entering the puppies to otter. A dog will certainly not be much use to otter hunters if he is loth to get his feet wet.

A strong, well-grown, male otter will weigh between 20 and 25 pounds, though enormous otters have been recorded. Few single terriers will therefore be able to best them in a duel. Irish dog fighters, who fought the morass of dogs that gave rise to the Irish terrier, the Kerry Blue terrier, the Wheaten terrier and the Glen of Imaal terriers, rated the otter highly, and there are tales of these large dogs killing otter, though it would be a very sad-looking terrier that survived such a battle. Conlan, a contemporary of Alys Serrell, owned a soft-coated Wheaten terrier that, in 1895, tackled and killed a 30-pound otter, only to die himself two weeks later from his wounds. Conlan's grandson still owns the stuffed dog, which was so highly esteemed that the family paid a taxidermist a fair price to have the beast mounted.

Clearly, the average Jack Russell terrier, weighing in at 14 pounds, give or take a pound or so, has no chance of mastering this creature in a fight. Terriers, however, are priceless allies during an otter hunt, for otters, when pushed, enter drains or seek refuge in holts or lairs beneath the roots of waterside trees. Thus a terrier will, by dint of barking and snapping, shift these otters to allow the hunt to pursue them. It is a popular belief that, while terriers enter quite readily to fox and badger, terriers are usually reluctant to enter to otter. Maybe it is difficult to create the necessary antipathy that will lead a dog to enter to otter, but my theory is that it is more likely because of the watery conditions present when entering takes place, rather than anything odd about the nature of the otter. A dog that will enter to quarry like a lion on *terra firma* might be just a little reluctant to chance his luck in two feet of water. Still, it is not difficult to enter a terrier once he has seen an otter being worked by another dog.

I must confess I've had some quite bad turns with otter. When I first came to my present abode, a mile from the usually otterless River Thame, I owned a grand little worker called Sly, a none too judicious blend of the terriers of my native mining valley and a granddaughter of Joan Begbie's Seale Cottage Welcome (reputedly one of the hardest terriers of the strain). Sly was, besides being lethal with fox, the supreme riverside ratter. She would scratch at a hole, race to the bolt, scratch again and bolt her rat, whereupon she would dive like a seal to field it. There were unusual floods the year I came, and such conditions throw rats out of kilter and get them off territory, making them easier for the kill. Thus, one Saturday in winter, I set out with a girl friend who was a ciné camera addict, with a view to filming Sly in her amazing aquatic acrobatics. The river was high, high enough to cover the land drains which open into the Thame, and for an hour or so we filmed Sly in her amazing dives, even getting a few shots of her emerging, rat in mouth, fruitlessly trying to kill the rat while she was still treading water, which, incidentally, is a very difficult task for a terrier to accomplish.

As we neared the edge of the Coopers' stretch of river beyond which I had no permission to hunt, Sly gave one of her seal-like dives and failed to surface again. She was only a few feet from the bank, so I feared the worst – that she was trapped beneath some tree root, or the chill of the water might have caused some cardiac malfunction. Frantically, I leapt into the water – a foolish, pointless, gesture as I had no idea where the damned bitch had sunk, and for ten minutes or more paddled around waist deep in the icy river. She had apparently sunk without trace. I was, I admit, damn nigh in tears as I crawled out of the water on to the bank and shook the water from my thoroughly sodden clothes. Then, beneath my feet, I could hear Sly's screaming falsetto bark – a bark entirely misrepresentative of the family of villains who had bred her. I had only an iron prod and a short grafting spade, but within minutes was down to a drainage pipe, which I proceeded to smash with heavy pebbles. Sly was nose to nose with a large dog otter in the land drain, and in spite of her courage was getting the worst of the encounter. I snatched her out of the pipe, a difficult task as she was slippery with water and blood, and the otter flashed past me, diving into the swollen river Thame. James Brockley who was at my house at the time, helped me to staunch the copious bleeding as best he could, but Sly died before I could get her to a vet.

Piper Allen, a confident otter hunter, once said that when he heard his dog call on an otter he was as good as selling the otter's pelt. Hats off to Piper Allen. I have never been that confident, and I miss Sly. He was a heck of a useful terrier by any standards. Sadly, she left only one line of descendants, a litter of four puppies, all of which came to sticky ends. Two were crippled by a very virulent strain of distemper that hit my premises before they were old enough to inoculate, and two were stolen by tinkers and died shortly after recovery, for, contrary to old wives' tales, the itinerant population are not the most responsible of dog owners. It was a great shame really, as she had the unique nose which makes a terrier such a priceless worker. I still hunt her great-niece, a doddery old bitch called Beltane – doddery, but still with that unique nose. However, I digress again. A bad fault, I'm afraid, or a sign of senility, perhaps.

The Wildcat

Otters make fearsome foes, but they pale to insignificance before the next quarry: namely, the Scottish wildcat. Reader, I beg you forget the relationship with the hearthside skulker that most households are pleased to own – though it is madness to underestimate even the household moggy, for he can be a great battler. The Scottish wildcat, however, is a demon. Pennant, a keen and enthusiastic naturalist if not a hunter, eulogizes over the creature's ferocity. Two tales will prove the point. One is the legendary tale of the Barnburgh cat and man battle which I described in my book *The Working Terrier*, and the other a hideous story that I heard only a week before writing this. It appears that among the tribes of Romany folk, who crossed the Asian European border regardless of political boundaries, thieving is considered a heinous crime deserving an ugly punishment. The mis-

The real Scottish wildcat – a fearsome foe for any terrier.

creant is put in a huge sack with a live, fully grown wildcat and then left. I will not dwell on the outcome of the event, but it is curious to note that the Romans executed political traitors in a similar manner, adding a few other beasts to the already overcrowded sack. It would be interesting to check on the origin of this particularly barbarous custom.

Cats of any sort are fighters, more than prepared to sell each of their nine lives dearly in defence of territory or young; and, when brought to bay, they make nightmare opponents. The Scottish wild-cat is representative of his tribe, and perhaps the most savage of all the felines. The 'British tiger', Pennant calls him. He is larger than the domesticated cat, the females being as large as a neutered domes-ticated tom, and their heads are broader and more powerful; otherwise, they resemble the typical domesticated tabby cat. It is with tempera-ment that the differences begin. Scottish wildcats resist any form of training, remaining savage, capricious and intractable, even if bred in captivity. Clearly they are not the ancestors of the hearthside pet.

Dogs required to hunt these Scottish wildcats should, to use the terms of the trade, be 'good baying dogs', required to stand back and give tongue while the diggers trench towards the cacophony. Just occasionally, dogs learn to kill these cats without receiving too much of a mauling, even as some terriers learn to dispose of a fox without too many rips and tears. One Grampian-based Russell-type terrier, bred by Will O'Donnell, is a famous wildcat slayer, and though the dog bears numerous scars, they are scarcely commensurate with the number of cats it has tackled. In most places, the wildcat is considered to be quite simply a nuisance, a disposable pest, for lamb-killing, fawn-killing, poultry-stealing cats are fairly common. It seems unlikely that this cat will receive any protection within the next few years, and such beasts provide easily obtained, exciting, though damnably dangerous quarry.

6   RABBIT HUNTING

The reader must obviously be curious as to why I have set out the subject of rabbit hunting as a separate chapter. Quite simply, rat, stoat, and to a lesser extent coypu hunting must be regarded as a training, a preparation for more dangerous quarry, namely fox, badger and otter. Rabbit hunting, however, is not preparatory. In fact it has a decidedly deleterious effect on a terrier that is to be entered to fox, and the reason is obvious if one examines the history of the typical fox or badger earth.

Most earths start their lives as enlarged rabbit warrens, and foxes and badgers breed quite happily in the large galleries of the warrens, while the unhappy, original tenants continue, for a while at least, to inhabit the small passages leading off the main entrances. Whether or not the sub-tenancy of these earths is as terrifying as one might imagine is open to question. Country legend has it that foxes and badgers will not kill the rabbits that inhabit these galleries. Fanciful, a pretty tale perhaps, but, to assume that such creatures practice such selection, such magnificent discrimination, is a bit ridiculous – as ridiculous, in fact, as the theory that lions will not harm grazing beasts drinking at the common waterhole; not only unlikely, but utterly fantastic. Still, rabbits will live for quite a time in earths that house foxes and badger.

In 1977, Dr Henry Clamp and I dug a fox in a well-established badger earth known to have held badgers for at least fifty years or more. During the excavation, which took twenty-nine hours, we dug through several rabbit passageways and we bolted quite a few rabbits by the noise of the dig. Now, dogs used to hunting rabbit may quite easily go to ground on fox and, when they are tired of baying at their foe, or, more likely, after a bit of a beating from a fox or a badger, will maybe transfer their attentions from fox to rabbit. There are people who tell you that their dogs hunt bunnies quite furiously above ground, but are rock steady to rabbit when hunting fox. I would dearly like such a dog, but have never owned one, nor, indeed, have I seen one . . . nor has anyone else, if my guess is correct. A dog used to hunt rabbit is always very unsteady to bunnies below ground and will transfer its attention to rabbits at a moment's notice. Thus, hunt terriers need to be broken to rabbit to be of any use for fox hunting, for reasons I have dealt with quite adequately earlier (pages 58–9).

Even so, rabbiting is usually good fun, and it is not everyone's wish to hunt fox. The traditional terrier man is no doubt throwing up his hands in horror, as well he may, but it is not everyone who has a chance to hunt foxes in number, or readily, nor who has the inclination in the case of many women dog owners. But the rabbit can be found in a variety of locations, and offers even the townie a chance to try his dog at some hunting. A dog which would otherwise go unhunted, I may add. There is a frightful mystique, a sort of curious snob appeal, about saying that one's dogs are bred only for fox. Maybe they are, but I know of two young ladies who use their terriers to hunt rabbits in my lane, and although the number of kills are small, the dogs are superbly trained and put the majority of hunt terriers to shame in the training area. I repeat, if rabbits are available, they provide excellent sport for the casual terrier owner.

Next fallacy to debunk, and quickly. Recently I met a young lady with a smart-looking team of Jack Russells. I stopped to look at them, and she, sensing my enthusiasm, came up with the 'sporting parson' spiel, the sort of sales talk that is repeated *ad nauseam* these days, and then added, for good measure, 'Of course, they were bred to go to ground and drive out rabbits.' It would have been a little rude of me to contradict her, but it was, to say the least, all rather ridiculous. A story will illustrate my point. Miniature dachshunds are often very sporting little dogs, and while the larger variety was bred to hunt badger – a task they will still do, incidentally – Forsyth of the Warwick Hunt proved beyond doubt that the smaller type was used as a rabbit-hunting dog. Some of these mites are very small, and will still flash into earths, quite unaware of the fact that the Kennel Club has reputedly ruined them. Even so, I have never seen a dachshund actually crawl up to a rabbit and bolt it, as would a ferret. Many might well dig their ways up the galleries to the rabbits – a highly dangerous task, as one might imagine, for a dog can suffocate easily in a rabbit warren – but they find it quite impossible to squeeze where a two and a half pound bunny has just gone. Lucas, out to exploit the sporting potential of any dog, wrote to a chap breeding these tiny dachshunds and received a photograph of one alongside a live rabbit. The dachshund was smaller, but, on examination, the rabbit was a domesticated one, and as 22-pound rabbits have been bred from time to time, it rather takes the gilt off the gingerbread of the story. Terriers may dig out rabbits, but are not usually capable of going down a warren and flushing them. The smallest working Jack Russell I have ever seen was bred by Miss Joan Begbie. It was a diminutive seven and a half inch little creature with a really fiery temper and game as a bantam cock. Even this mite could not get up to the average rabbit lying up in the typical rabbit warren.

What use are terriers for rabbit hunting, then? The answer is that they are of considerable use. Terriers used for rabbit hunting can be divided into three categories, though some terriers will fulfil all these three requirements, and fairly adequately at that.

1. Ferreting dogs.
2. Bushing dogs.
3. Rough-and-ready gun dogs.

Ferreting Dogs

Terriers can be quite easily trained to work with ferrets, provided, as we said earlier, that the dog comes to regard the ferret as an ally and not a creature to be attacked or killed. Breaking grown terriers, particularly dogs that have killed rats and stoats, to ferret is, to put it mildly, hell's delight. I have broken maybe a hundred grown dogs to ferret, though I must admit it is a task I do not enjoy. Puppies really are easy to get accustomed to ferrets, however. I have already dealt with the gentling process (page 35), so will not continue to dwell on the subject here. The terrier should be absolutely obedient to make it an efficient ferreting dog, and one which races about, throwing the net, allowing rabbits to escape, or, worse still, snapping at rabbits while still in the net, is a great pest.

My own ferreting dog, Set, a superb rabbiter and one of the most intelligent terriers I ever owned, used to hold netted rabbits with her feet whenever they became so lively as to throw the nets and escape, whereas any rabbit who missed the nets and tried to make a run for it was snapped up and killed. Greg Mouseley, whose rough dog, Rastus, appears on page 18, mentions that one of his own dogs has also acquired this habit. It requires an enormous amount of work to produce such a dog, and few of these dogs are ever sold, even by the omnipresent dog dealers who specialize in the sales of semi-trained dogs. Set was a delight to own. She caught her first rabbit when she was just twelve weeks of age, crawling after it into an old fox earth. She dug for maybe an hour to get to it, and killed it with her milk teeth. As she grew older, she became so dextrous at ferreting that she would deliberately find an unnetted hole under cover, a hole so small I'd failed to notice it, and crouch like a cat, her tail wagging with excitement. As a fox dog, she was damn-nigh useless – no coward, mind you, but she would change quarry as soon as she sniffed a rabbit in the earth and ignore the fox she had encountered. Horses for courses, though, and her haul of rabbits would not have disgraced a lurcher. Sadly, she was very inbred to my old line, a line rich in bitches that died from hypercalcaemia, and as luck would have it she died too.

It took two years to train her, and ten minutes to lose her, and I felt her loss deeply.

Without wishing to boast, I have only ever seen one dog to better Set at rabbiting, and that was a near-senile Border terrier owned by Nap Johnson. To acquire such skills requires years of training, far more training than it requires to produce a dog to go down an earth and simply bark at, or kill, a fox, yet, curiously, fox-hunting dogs usually fetch a better price than a dog skilled at rabbiting. Possibly the truth is that few really good rabbiting dogs are offered for sale.

Bushing Dogs

Bushing dogs is a term used in the Midlands to describe dogs that work cover to catch rabbits, bottling them up in tangles of roots and briars, or quite simply to bolt them for whippets or lurchers to catch. In spite of the terrier's lack of speed, and no Jack Russell is capable of outrunning an adult rabbit, this is a very efficient method of tackling rabbits in woodland or very thick undergrowth. Some terriers will smash through

A rabbit bolt hole: practically invisible to the human eye, but easily detected by the first class rabbiting terrier.

covers so thick that it would deter even a springer spaniel, but a fairly powerful type of terrier is fairly essential for the job. Lucas took hundreds of rabbits by 'bushing' woodland with his team of Sealyhams.

Teams of terriers are best for the task if lurchers are not being used to catch the bolting rabbits, for the very sound of numerous terriers crunching their way noisily through the brambles panics, or disorientates, the rabbit either into squatting in the hope it will not be seen, or into doing something very stupid like running for cover so thick that it cannot escape from the tangles. Noisy terriers are often better bushing dogs than silent ones, as the barking tends really to drive the rabbit to do something stupid. In the United States, small teams of beagles are used to hunt cottontails and imported British rabbits, and Drayton, who has done considerable work on the science of hunting with hounds – his book, I believe, is forthcoming in 1981 – is of the opinion that the success of the beagle as a rabbiting dog is partly the result of its unerring nose, and partly the result of the fact that the beagle is so garrulous that rabbits are really panicked by the non-stop baying of the scent-hunting beagle. A difficult theory to prove, but I, for one, am ready to believe it.

Rough-and-Ready Gun Dogs

As a shooting dog, the Russell is very useful providing, and this is a big proviso I must admit, that it can be kept very close and very, very obedient. Breed loyalty aside, for such loyalty is most unscientific, Russells are perhaps the brightest of terriers, but this, too, is a bit of a dubious distinction, since the terrier is no canine genius, no matter what its proud owner may insist. Furthermore, most terriers with good noses are so besotted by the scent they are hunting that they run deaf; that is to say, when they are on a hot trail they are totally engrossed in the chase, so engrossed that they often cannot be called off the scent. To train a springer, labrador or collie to come off the trail is easy, or moderately easy, but it is a devil of a job to call off the average Russell.

Colin Willock, whose entertaining book *Dudley, the Worst Dog in the World* is a must for anyone who has fought a losing battle with a semi-gun-trained terrier, gives interesting accounts of the failings of his terrier as a gun dog. To be very honest, in thirty-five years of terrier training I have only ever had one very obedient terrier; only one who would work to gun and come off the scent, drop to shot, point and retrieve. Not a very good record, I must admit, but a terrier is, quite simply, not a spaniel, and certainly not tractable enough to compete with retrieving dogs, no matter what some foolish books about the breed state. Nevertheless, terriers are the best dogs I have ever seen for facing very thick cover, and most have a will to go on in places where most dogs would certainly jib.

Some years ago I buried my veteran terrier, San, and it damned near broke my heart. In his twenty-one years he performed every task I asked of him, and not only was he a wizard to fox, but he would retrieve shot pigeons out of cover so deep that a child could walk across the top of the brambles. He took every form of game, even woodcock, that was foolish enough to squat in cover while he ploughed through. But such a dog is not only a rarity among terriers, it requires many years of work to produce. I think it was Jack London who said that, by the time a dog was old enough to do every task, it was too damned old to do any task. An iron will is necessary to train a terrier to the gun, and many are the heartaches. Still, I have trained one, so every beginner can take heart.

Rabbits are today certainly making a comeback, in spite of man's efforts to exterminate them. One of the earliest references to the humble bunny is, in fact, a letter sent to the Emperor Augustus by the irate citizens of the Balearic Islands, asking the emperor to send a legion of troops to prevent the islands becoming bankrupt through the rabbit damage to the vineyards. Augustus declined, but when rabbits do become numerous they can certainly be a heck of a problem. In dry conditions, ten rabbits will eat more than a sheep, and as rabbits are inclined to browse more than they graze, they destroy far more than they eat. Furthermore, a healthy, average rabbit defecates and urinates in certain definite areas, one rabbit producing about 360 pellets a day and a corresponding amount of acidic urine. Therefore it is not long before the fetid patches become rank and unsuitable for vegetation other than spurry and similar inedible plants.

In Laysan Island, nearly all the vegetation was destroyed by the rabbits, and in 1923 Alexander Whetmore visited the spot and saw only a few survivors of a vast colony whose anti-social behaviour had caused the near-extinction of the species. Gassing, ferreting, hunting all failed to destroy Laysan's rabbit population, for it should be mentioned that in any predator-free area like Laysan, one pair of rabbits will produce 70,000 offspring in two years. I must admit that, as a hunter, I really enjoy the presence of the rabbit, though if I were a farmer I would probably hate them. However, both farmers and hunters alike were appalled by the introduction of myxomatosis in 1953, a disease which nearly exterminated the rabbit in Britain. Hundreds of dead rabbits littered the road and fields, and blind and deranged bunnies rushed blindly about the countryside. The rabbit is now making a comeback, I feel, and unless some scientist comes up with another sickening panacea, twenty years will see rabbits back in number once again, and maybe providing excellent sport for the terrier keeper who disdains being a purist.

7 BREEDING

There are few genuine dog enthusiasts who do not try their hand at dog breeding at some time or another. Not only is breeding an entertaining and interesting hobby, but it does offer a chance to improve on the stock one possesses. It is a true saying that, if you want a really good dog, you must breed it yourself. Few rival terrier breeders/owners will sell you their best. There are some professional dog breeders who can make money out of their dogs, but these are few and far between, and the way some of them 'cut corners' regarding feeding and rearing often merit prosecution. If the tiro dog breeder even clears his expenses, then he will usually be very lucky indeed. To be brief, if you are looking for an interesting, exciting, educating hobby, this could be it, but do not expect to make a fortune by breeding terriers.

A bitch terrier puppy will normally come into season at between six and nine months of age, the later time being the more common. Few serious terrier breeders breed from their first-season bitches for a variety of reasons, however. First, this is the time when the puppy should be experiencing the introduction to quarry, not the pleasures of parenthood. A break in the training period at this critical time is not advantageous. Secondly, many bitches are woefully juvenile at this age, and some are literally bewildered at the sensation of giving birth to puppies. Many, though I should stress not all, will be a bit indifferent to the plight of the puppies, and I have known many juvenile bitches totally reject their litters. Puppy mortalities are invariably quite high in the offspring when a bitch is mated before she is a year old, and this position is considerably worse in the bigger breeds, who are not only slower developing physically, but are also very mentally juvenile under two years old. Many sight hounds do not come into season until they are two years old anyway and perhaps it is the Almighty's way of making sure that the young, silly bitches are not forced into premature puppy bearing.

On the other side of the scales, it should be pointed out that there is a school of thought which advocates the first season mating and bearing of puppies. This school of thought, and a great many sensible, scientific American dog breeders believe in first-season mating, argues that when a bitch is immature her pelvic bones are soft, and thus the birth of the puppies is rarely as traumatic as it would be when the pelvis is not as pliable as in an older bitch. Furthermore, these breeders argue, even if the bitch loses her first litter through lack of maternal instinct, the experience will serve her well enough during future whelping. It is a matter of debate, but not here, I feel. Let me debunk another popular fallacy, however. Many breeders will tell the inexperienced terrier man that a bitch mated in her first season, who conceives and bears a litter from this early mating, is ruined for life, since the mating, pregnancy, whelping and rearing has the effect of preventing the bitch growing properly to maturity. It simply isn't so. Research done into this old wives' tale has shown that bitches who have bred litters in their first season grow to a similar height and weight as their maiden siblings.

Personally, I do not like first-season matings, as at that time a bitch hasn't had the opportunity to prove her worth, to show that she is worthy of perpetuating a blood line. She has scarcely had time to test her mettle against rat, let alone heavier quarry, and good nose (a prime requisite in a working terrier) has not had time to manifest itself at this tender age. If the breeder merely wishes to produce puppies, then there is nothing wrong with first-season matings. If he intends to perpetuate the useful qualities of a strain, to breed only the best, then it is far too early to mate the bitch, since she is as unproven in the hunting field as she is at litter bearing.

Most bitches come into season twice a year, though once a year is not uncommon, and this is often the case in the bigger breeds. What actually brings a bitch into season at these times is largely conjecture, and little serious research has been done on the subject. Goodall and Van Lawick, in their magnificent book *Innocent Killers*, a study which is a must for any serious dog breeder or hunter, opens up a new field of thought on this subject, and while it must be pointed out that these researches were conducted on Cape hunting dogs, which are not true dogs, and jackals, which may according to Lorenz be true dogs, the authors' ideas probably hold good for all canines.

Light is apparently a most important factor in determining when a bitch will come into season, but again, I must emphasize, little research has been done on the subject. Whole families of terriers seem to come into season just once a year, so perhaps the characteristic of coming into season during certain set months is inherited. My own strain of terriers are once-a-year season bitches, and as I am not a commercial breeder and hunt a mixed team, I am grateful for the peculiarity. Some years ago I had a very fecund bitch called Colt, which came into season every four months, and, what was worse, experienced phantom pregnancies every time she was unmated. The ideal bitch for the commercial terrier breeder perhaps, but a hell of a nuisance for the hunter with a mixed team of terriers.

Normally bitches will begin to show when they are near season by the area of the vagina 'twixt tail and vaginal orifice becoming swollen. Many are extremely skittish about this time, and sometimes display marked disobedience to command. Eventually, the vagina widens and a few drops of bloody fluid are passed. The purpose of this bloody fluid is a bit obscure, for few wild dogs manifest such symptoms when they are ready to receive the mate. A few years ago, one biologist put forward the idea that it was a domesticated bitch's way of showing its owner that it was ready for mating. This is specu- lation, however – interesting speculation, perhaps, but scarcely provable. At this stage a bitch becomes sexually exciting to dogs, who will usually try to ride her. Some bitches endure this fruitless court- ship in a resigned fashion, while others savagely repel other dogs' advances.

While the bloody discharge is still copious, few bitches will allow a dog to mate, however. Towards the twelfth day of season, the dis- charge will have almost ceased and the vagina will be very distended and swollen. Many bitches will turn their tail aside for any dog at this time, and some will actually take the sexual courtship to the dog, riding him and displaying obviously male characteristics to excite his libido. Such animals are now ready for mating. Reader, please do not take the twelfth day of season as being gospel for the time when every bitch will mate. If sexual cycles in mammals were all that predictable, there would no doubt be a large number of pedigree dogs in existence and very few Catholics in this crowded world. Just as every woman has a different sexual metabolism, so has every bitch. I have known bitches who would stand for mating at the second and third day of season and conceive from a mating during these times. Likewise, I have known, and still have, a bitch who refuses to stand until the twenty-third day of season. However, when a bitch is obviously interested in dogs and turns her tail, inviting attention of male dogs, she is usually ready to mate, and then she is also most likely to conceive.

Let us now deal with the stud dog and his function in the alliance. Usually the male terrier is ready for mating at a year old, though stories of six-month-old puppies who have served their dams are a dime a dozen. When a terrier's testicles have descended into the scrotum, he is normally fertile, and though dogs with testicles still held in their body will mate and tie, I have never known such a union to be fertile. A young stud mated for the first time can often be a very infuriating animal to the breeder and the bitch it is hoped he will mate. He will frequently try to mate the bitch for hours, riding her head, ejaculating semen prematurely and being a bit of a disappointment all round. For this reason, I would advise the breeder to take his maiden bitch to an experienced stud dog and not to an untried male just down the street.

First matings can be very maddening affairs, particularly if the male is as inexperienced as the female. Furthermore, dogs which have reached four or five years old before mating their first bitch make very, very inefficient, and often indifferent, studs, and some will try to serve a bitch till exhaustion overtakes them without succeeding in tying. Others totally ignore even the most passionate advances of the bitch. About five or six years ago I had a phone call from a would-be terrier breeder, asking if I had a stud dog that would serve his bitch. Duly he appeared on my doorstep with a tiny, timid, terrified animal who went berserk with fear when my stud dog appeared. She had good reason to be afraid – her vagina was so bruised and damaged that no stud dog could possibly mate her without her experiencing the most awful agony. It transpired that before this man had phoned me he had taken his bitch to numerous local, inexperienced dogs, all of which had tried to mate her, but all of which had only succeeded in bruising her vagina so badly she was totally incapable of tying with any dog during that particular season at least. The breeder with a maiden bitch should go to an experienced stud dog for the first mating, and a proven stud dog is in any case not only more capable of mating, but also guaranteed to be fertile.

Yet another old wives' tale to be dispelled: only a few months ago I read in one of the stereotyped dog manuals an account of how to manage a stud dog. Apparently, this good lady advised, the male should be mated at nine months of age, and then not used until he is eighteen months. Why, she did not explain, and I certainly cannot, for I am utterly bewildered at such advice. It certainly does not contain any biological reasoning. Once a dog is sexually mature he should be allowed to mate frequently. Once a day is not too often, provided (a) he is eager and not exhausted by his stud work, (b) he is not hurt or bruised by his sexual athletics. The reason for my statement? Well, the life of a healthy sperm is roughly seventy-two hours if kept within the body of the dog. Thus, a dog who mates irregularly passes a great number of dead sperm, or sperm reaching the end of their life cycle and no longer capable of fertilizing an ovum. A dog who mates regularly is usually a lot more fertile and has his semen full of viable sperm.

About ten years ago I owned a stud dog called Rupert, a neat little stud dog and game as a bantam cock. When he was fourteen months old and at his sexual prime, he developed what could only be called a passion for his grandmother. She was in season at the time, and he would go into paroxysms of rage when another dog went near her. I could not have asked for a more splendid subject to test my theory on fertility, for when he was denied mating her he refused his food and pined. On 3 August 1969, I mated him twelve times to his grand-dam, and each time he succeeded in tying. I then took out his granddam and allowed a bitch belonging to a biologist friend, a lady as interested in my theory as I was, to be mated by this dog just once. Thirteen matings in one day, and the second bitch also conceived. So much for the pseudo-science of dog breeding. Obviously it is not wise or purposeful to allow a dog to mate so frequently, but it certainly proved my point. There is a great deal of silly, unscientific hogwash written about dog breeding.

So to the actual act of mating. Assume that the bitch is ready to 'stand' – a term used by dog breeders to indicate sexual readiness – and is eager to accept the attentions of the dog. The male now mounts the bitch and, by a series of pelvic jerks, succeeds in pushing his penis into the bitch's vagina. During his final thrust, the hind legs of the stud usually leave the ground for a few seconds. Now, the peculiarity of the mating technique of nearly all (though not all) canines is that, as soon as the penis penetrates the bitch, the end of the said organ swells like a small golf ball, preventing the dog from withdrawing his penis. The dog then shifts his hind legs until he is back to back with the bitch. This position, which to the beginner must seem most incongruous, is what is known as 'a tie', and although it is not essential for a dog and a bitch to tie to conceive, it is usually necessary.

The tie is a biological mystery, and no one has come up with an explanation for it. In the wild it must leave the couple extremely vulnerable to attack from other predators and even their own kind, and only fear, pain or shock, or else completion of mating, will cause the penis to become flaccid so that the dog can withdraw. (Hence the bucket of water sometimes thrown over the couple by well-wishers.) I cannot therefore attempt to try and explain the purpose of the tie. I don't know why dogs tie, nor do I know of any competent cynologist who does. A tie can last for quite a long time. Twenty minutes is a usual time for a tie, but one dog, a rough-coated Jack Russell terrier male called Stealer, who belonged to Robert Turton of Birmingham, once tied for three hours to a bitch, and stories of frighteningly long ties are not uncommon in mastiffs and very large breeds.

Now for a spot of advice aimed at the owner of a stud dog. Some bitch owners will ask for the dog to mate a bitch naturally. By this they usually mean allowing the couple to run free, and while it must be admitted that such courtship is sometimes needed to get a bitch in the right humour to mate, it is also extremely dangerous. Let me explain why. When the end of the dog's penis begins to swell, it causes the bitch considerable discomfort, not to say pain. Many are in agony, and writhe and scream fit to wake the dead. It does a dog no good to be dragged around by his penis, and many an amateur street Lothario has been ruptured by these antics. Sometimes also a bitch will savage a dog during a mating, and I have had several stud dogs nipped during tying, but no tale I could tell could match the story told by a Walsall dog fighter during the turn of the century. A noted pit dog had killed four opponents in four fights – a horrid and vile record and, incidentally, a very rare record, for, in spite of stories to the contrary, few fights continued to the death. So he was put to stud. He mated a young bitch, who was quite young and very game, and after penetration she turned and savaged him so badly that his foreleg was a red ruin, eventually atrophying and falling off – an expensive price to pay for a natural mating. Thus it makes good sense to hold the bitch, or better still to get the owner to hold her after she has tied.

Some bitches resent strangers holding them during the mating, and will often snap at the hands that hold them. It is a standard joke that my left-hand fingers are broken as a result of a friend's bitch attacking them during a mating. It happened after I had received an inquiry about the use of a stud, and in due course a doctor from Birmingham appeared with a smart little white bitch. She was 'bad with people', I was told, but bravado on my part made me careless of advice. Alas, it was good advice, as I was to find out all too soon. As I held her for my stud to mount, she snapped at me and her teeth met through my cheek. It is extremely embarrassing, not to say painful, to need to have a dog's teeth prised out of one's face. Since then I have muzzled aggressive bitches by binding their jaws together with non-adhesive tape. I learn only by mistakes, it appears, and, reader, I have made many.

With the tie completed and the mating terminated, the dog withdraws his penis and the bitch sets to licking herself. Usually a small trickle of semen leaves the bitch. If I had a penny for every time I have seen some idiot lift the bitch, bottom in the air, to prevent the semen running out, I should be a rich man indeed. It is biologically totally unnecessary, though it has the merit of being amusing to watch. Some of the ideas that dog breeders hold are amazing. Here is just one of the absurd fallacies which infest dog breeding. The semen is surplus to requirements, and sufficient will be left in the fine capillary tubes adjoining the uterus to ensure conception. Even so, I know several apparently experienced dog breeders who go through this amazing ritual every time a bitch is mated. Don't do it – it is the hallmark of a moron. If you still wish to perform this antic, please contact me as I have friends who specialize in taking comic photographs.

Mating completed, away home with the bitch. Now, beware. Your bitch will still accept other suitors and can still conceive to other dogs. Mixed litters are not only possible but extremely likely if the female is mated by more than one dog. An example will illustrate the point. Some time ago a former girl friend of mine left her Siamese cat while she returned to her medical practice in the West Indies. Female Siamese, of course, come into season regularly, and when they do they call fit to wake the dead. So noisy was she that I would put her in a box, drive with her to a field half a mile from my cottage, and here leave both box and car and go back to sleep in my cottage. In summertime, moreover, Siamese cats come into season every few weeks, so in desperation I took her to be mated to a famous Siamese stud. On fetching her home, I opened the box, and she at once flashed out of the window to some feral half-wild toms who were always in attendance around the house – one a black one-eyed monster who killed fowl, another a ginger tom who had been left behind when a neighbour moved. Nine weeks later my female kittened. In her litter were two Siamese, one ginger as well as one black which fortunately had both its eyes. Mixed litters are common in badly run kennels where bitches are allowed to roam at will, and, remember, your bitch will still be frantic to get out of the house to her boy friend, even after she has been served by a stud of your choice. Keep her up at least three weeks after she's been mated, and, reader, that can be quite a task, for a bitch will often be frantic to be mated regularly during her season.

We can assume by now that the bitch has conceived. By four or five weeks after the mating she will certainly show all the signs of pregnancy. Her teats will begin to swell, and her belly and chest will show definite cleavage as the mammary glands begin to swell out with milk to support the forthcoming litter. Here is a timely piece of common-sense advice – a rare commodity in books on dog breeding, I'm afraid. A wild, pregnant canine female usually hunts by herself. Wolves are the exception, not the rule, so, as pregnancy proceeds, the female becomes heavier, more ungainly, and therefore less able to hunt. Thus the wild female receives less food than she would before she was mated – note: *less food during pregnancy, not more*. Bitches are prepared for this, and as a rule the body of the bitch makes allowances for the lean times ahead. Bitches in season lay up stores of fat around vital organs, particularly around the heart (it is for this reason that greyhound bitches are not allowed to run on licensed tracks just prior to, and after, receiving). In addition to this strange fact, the alimentary canal of the bitch becomes far more efficient. Dogs are notoriously wasteful feeders, and much of the protein in the food passes through the dog undigested. In the pregnant bitch, the alimentary tract becomes more efficient and absorbs more of the protein than it would in the days prior to pregnancy.

Thus a bitch carrying puppies needs *ad lib* feeding like it needs a hole in the head, and, believe me, both are equally dangerous. Gorging a bitch is positively asking for trouble. Not only does the pregnant bitch become fat and sluggish on such a diet, but her puppies become over-large and thus, at the end of the pregnancy, a fat, ill-conditioned, bitch is forced with the delivery of ridiculously overweight puppies – and the result is often disastrous. For the first seven weeks of pregnancy, the bitch requires no extra food; and for the final few weeks, only small amounts of extra. As her abdomen becomes distended, the stomach is obviously less able to cope with one huge meal, so several smaller meals a day should be offered.

Don't – and this is a big don't – feed masses of extra calcium in the form of either calcium lactate or calcium oleate. Calcium lactate is not usually properly absorbed and causes the faeces to become cemented into a chalk-like mass, creating awful constipation, while feeding soluble calcium salts increases the chances of hypercalcaemia during the rearing of the puppies. More on that topic later. A dog's diet should be primarily meat – personally, I believe all meat, though this is disputed by a great many eminent authorities, and a bitch who is fed a rich meat diet during pregnancy will not benefit from masses of extra unnatural chemical nourishment. I have never used supplementary feeds for pregnant bitches, and I have reared quite a number of puppies in my time. A good rule should be to feed the very pregnant bitch frequent, small and very nourishing meals, and to keep well away from chemical vitamin supplements. I'm not a 'back to nature' freak, though I have already confessed that I went through this phase at one time in my life, but I think man relies far too heavily on chemical feeds.

Some fifty-eight to sixty-three days after mating (a small dog sometimes has a somewhat shorter gestation period than a large one), a bitch will start to whelp. Watch her carefully towards the end of her time. Sometimes bitches with large litters will be unable to break down the toxic waste which the foetuses are passing into her blood along the placenta – waste produced not only by herself but by the puppies. This toxaemia, which is the failure of the liver to cope with the extra waste, can be very dangerous indeed. A listless, pregnant bitch without appetite is always suspect and needs careful veterinary treatment if she is to survive. Fortunately, toxaemia is fairly rare in terrier bitches.

Assuming a normal pregnancy and a normal birth, however, we will leave the abnormalities to be dealt with later. A bitch near to parturition will seek a place to whelp and will act in an anxious manner. Bitches whelping for the first time become frantic, while older bitches accept the birth of puppies almost phlegmatically. Most bitches will scratch at the floor of their whelping boxes madly, and, if the box is lined with newspaper (the best whelping material, actually), she will render the paper to ribbons. One bitch Saluki belonging to Arthur Smith of Walsall dug up the brick of his shed to whelp her puppies. While such frantic scratching looks distressing, one should not under any circumstances try to stop or restrain the bitch. Again, such an action has a biological purpose. The violent exertion has the effect of stimulating the pituitary gland to produce hormones that will cause the bitch's pelvis to widen and make way for the forthcoming birth of the puppies.

Some years ago, a lady from Birmingham phoned me and, after a few panic-stricken mumbles and tears, stated that her bitch was tearing up the paper and was having to be restrained by actually being put in a home-made straitjacket affair. Restraint is dangerous. Allow nature to take its course – for the moment, at least. Just before the actual birth begins, the bitch becomes relatively calm – a preparatory stage for the violent exertions to come; and, make no mistake about it, the birth of a litter is a very taxing business for a bitch. Some bitches become extraordinarily thirsty and take in large quantities of water, but few will consider food at this time.

The bitch's uterus now begins to contract, and some straining is fairly obvious. After a short period varying between a few minutes to maybe half an hour, a membranous bag full of clear liquid begins to emerge from the bitch's vagina. This bag is now followed by yet another membranous sac, this time containing a bitter, greenish fluid. Try not to excite the bitch or to encourage her to break these sacs. The fluid within the bags acts as a kind of lubricant, allowing the puppies to slide into the world. Should these sacs become ruptured, releasing the fluids, a dry delivery and an unlubricated birth is inevitable. This will be far more traumatic for both the bitch and the puppies than a normal delivery. The puppy is now forced down the vagina by the contractions of the uterus, and the extra exertion usually ruptures the bags, releasing the puppy into a world where it is forced to breath air for the first time in its life. Sometimes the sac does not rupture, however, and experienced whelpers will lick the sacs violently to release the puppy. The bitch will also lick the puppy frantically after its release from the sac-like prison.

This licking is purposeful, for it stimulates the respiratory and vascular system much in the same way that a sharp smack on the new-born baby's bottom causes it to cry out and inhale its first mouthful of air. As a matter of interest, bears lick their new-born with a sort of crazy enthusiasm to get the semi-comatose cubs to breathe. The ancients believed that the bear was actually licking the cub into its shape, much as a sculptor sculpts stone into a figure – and hence the term 'licking into shape' entered the English language.

Let us return from the realms of folklore to the world of canine midwifery, however. More often than not, the puppy is born head first, and this is a biologically sound method, for the delivery takes a fair time and there is at least a chance that the head will be clear of the birth canal and perhaps – and it is a big perhaps – able to breathe air if the sacs of fluid are ruptured. My own theory for this curious birth position, and most mammals are born head first, is that the head of the mammal is the hardest part of the body, and it is the head which clears the way in the birth canal so that the body might follow unhindered by muscular obstruction. Yet some people are shocked when puppies are born feet first, though, contrary to many theories, it is fairly common and should give no reason for alarm. Nearly half of my own puppies were born feet first, and provided the birth is not a protracted one, no harm occurs to the puppies or the bitch.

The dreaded breach position is just a little different from the straightforward, feet-first delivery. Sometimes birth is protracted and the bitch is faced with the position of having a puppy hanging half out of her body. This frequently panics a maiden bitch, though an experienced bitch has little fear about it. In this event, grip the puppy in rough towelling, for it is too slippery to be held 'in any other material, and ease the puppy out of the bitch, working with the contractions of the mother. The puppy has now left the sanctuary of the bitch for a somewhat hostile and chilly world, which brings us to a highly controversial subject.

The bitch's body temperature is roughly 101.5 °F, and in this constant temperature the foetus has spent the past nine weeks. It is now pushed forth into a world unlike the sterile, warm environment it has hitherto known; into a world where temperatures are considerably below that of the womb. The shock of birth must be fairly traumatic to all animals, and to be born into a chilly environment is certainly not helpful to the development of the puppy. Heat is fairly essential if the puppy is to survive and grow apace. The heat can be provided by whelping the litter in a warm room, or, if the bitch whelps outside, by hanging some heating device, such as an infra-red lamp, above the litter. There are, on the other hand, many terrier breeders who scoff at the use of heat lamps, stating that the weak and sickly puppies don't survive if the bitch is whelped in a cold shed. It is a fascinating piece of logic. The trouble with it is that it just isn't logical. In a cold shed, even the strongest puppy who crawls away from his dam, or is hurled from the nest when his dam leaves to feed or defaecate, chills and dies, or checks in growth. The breeder who advocates such Spartan treatment is either plain ignorant of the needs of the puppy, or quite simply too mean to speculate on a heating device.

The Dog Breeders Act of 1973 stipulates that heat shall be provided for newly born whelps, and unless the weather is near-tropical, artificial heat is needed. A bitch which whelps in mid-winter will not rear her puppies properly unless artificial heat is provided. Puppies born and reared in chilly conditions are easily recognizable. Most have pot-bellies, thin coats and fleshless ribs, no matter how they are fed. In 1970, I had the misfortune to visit the dreadful itinerants' site at Slacky Lane, Pelsall, a veritable Dachau of dog breeding, and the sight of the pitiful puppies reared in those dreadful conditions is still in my memory. I frequently bite my tongue to prevent comment when I hear some fool say that the best dogs one can buy are from itinerants. A visit to the now disbanded tinker site at Slacky Lane, Pelsall, would have convinced even the most ill-informed of such sages of the untruths in their statements. Heat is essential if one is to rear puppies properly.

Some bitches take a considerable time to whelp their puppies – most books tell you that the puppies are born at half-hour intervals. This is not true. Few creatures give birth with such clockwork precision. Some bitches take a full day to whelp. Others complete the job in a matter of two hours. I once owned a bitch called Blackface who came into season just once a year, but who whelped with incredible ease. No sooner had she licked her first puppy clean of foetal fluid than the second made its appearance into the world. She once whelped a litter of five puppies in under an hour. Not all bitches whelp that easily, though. Blackface's mother, a tan-and-white bitch called Jade, often took twenty hours to produce her litter. Very long waits between puppies, however, should cause the breeder some concern, particularly when the bitch is inexperienced and has never produced a litter before. A good rule is: if in doubt, don't hesitate, get expert advice. And by expert advice I mean a vet, not the old man down the road who has whelped a few litters during his days as a dog breeder.

Expert help is certainly needed if things go wrong, and things can go wrong, believe me. Statistics tend to show that parturition problems are more frequent when small breeds whelp than when large breeds give birth to puppies. Jack Russell terriers are small dogs, and whereas it would be ridiculous to suggest that the breed is prone to whelping difficulties, as are bulldogs, or chihuahuas, whelping problems are, nevertheless, not infrequent. The most common cause of whelping difficulties is simply uterine inertia, or, in layman's terms, simply a tired womb. After a difficult and lengthy delivery (the delivery of a large puppy can be very tiring, and sometimes takes quite a time), the bitch may be so exhausted that she finds the birth of the next puppy too demanding. Thus the contractions of the womb grow weak and feeble, and cannot push the puppy down the birth canal.

For heaven's sake, forget about such witchcraft remedies as syrup of figs or castor oil during such emergencies. If the bitch is in obvious difficulties, get her to a vet and get her there promptly. More often than not, the problem can be rectified by an injection of calcium salt that peps up the tired uterus just enough to get the puppy pushed out of the uterus into the birth canal. Failing this, the vet resorts to another chemical called pituitrin. This causes more severe contractions of the womb, and usually works very quickly, within half an hour of injection.

My ancient brood bitch, Wen, was nine when she produced her last litter (a quick boast, if I may: she bred forty-six working certificated offspring). She was a bit old for whelping, I know, but I was tempted to mate her one last time as she bred such incredibly good puppies. After one puppy had been born, Wen simply gave up, and I watched the feeble contractions for a few minutes before getting her to the vet. The injection of the calcium salt had no effect, as it rarely does if a bitch is in her dotage, and I prepared myself for a Caesarian operation. However, she responded rapidly to pituitrin and produced three puppies in eleven minutes, all on the floor of my van during the return journey to my cottage. A word of warning, though, pituitrin is not a substance to be administered by a layman, and as an aid to parturition it is always a little risky. A lady doctor friend described it as like adjusting a carburettor with a sledge hammer. A carefully regulated injection of the substance usually has the required results, but it invariably leaves the bitch feeling as weak as water. Furthermore, an injection of pituitrin given to a bitch with a pelvic deformity, administered illegally by a layman, may actually cause contractions that split the uterus, forcing the contents into the alimentary tracts. Pituitrin is not a substance to be administered by amateurs.

Sometimes, of course, it does not have the required effect, and the veterinary surgeon must resort to a Caesarian section. That is, the abdomen and the womb must be opened and the puppies brought into the world through an incision. One of the Roman Caesars was born by this method, hence the word Caesarian. Before the reader gasps in horror at the prospect of such an operation, literally nearly disembowelling his bitch, may I say that the operation is quite simple for a skilled veterinary surgeon and that the puppies are usually home and dry within half an hour of the operation commencing. Very few bitches indeed die of this operation, though a few puppies have been known to die through the trauma of such an unnatural entry into the world. In fact, however, one American veterinary surgeon has put forward a notion that the dangers of a Caesarian are smaller than the dangers of a normal birth. A Caesarian is certainly not as exhausting as a lengthy natural delivery, so long as, of course, the bitch is not exhausted by fruitless straining. Vets are usually a bit reluctant to perform Caesarian sections on toxaemic bitches as the liver of the toxaemic animal is usually so full of injurious substances that the liver has difficulty breaking down the anaesthetic required during the Caesarian section. Even so, a Caesarian section should not terrify the novice dog breeder, though such an operation may be a little expensive, I must add, about the price of one puppy.

Delivery over, either natural or assisted by Caesarian section, we may move on to the next stage. For the first day or so after delivery, the bitch is usually a bit reluctant to leave her puppies, and some bitches are even more reluctant to eat. Normally she will have eaten the trappings of birth, namely the amnion, the chorion (the two membranous sacs that enclose the foetus) and the placenta. She is probably feeling a little under the weather after such apparently unnatural viands, but unnatural they are not, in fact, and the bitch should not be prevented from eating the unsavoury-looking mess. Many veterinary surgeons believe that the ingestion of the two sacs and the placenta stimulates the milk flow of the bitch (a difficult theory to prove, perhaps), while others believe that these birth trappings help to clean out the alimentary tract in the mother. Black, or greeny-black faeces are usually passed the day after delivery as a result of the ingestion of this waste. Bitches denied the right of eating these trappings (bitches having Caesarian sections, for example) certainly don't seem to suffer too much from the loss, but perhaps the ingestion of the messy substances is not as necessary as some veterinarians believe. Yet, when a natural birth has occurred, the bitch should be allowed to eat the sacs and placenta.

The first few days after birth, the puppies suckle a yellow milky fluid called colostrum or first milk. This milk, called beastings in cows, is extremely valuable. Not only is it considerably richer than the actual dog's milk, but it also contains antibodies, substances that allow puppies to fight the various diseases that beset dogs, diseases to which the bitch has acquired immunity and can therefore pass on this immunity to the puppies via the colostrum. It is also a little-known fact that dogs, cats and ferrets are among the few animals that receive these antibodies across the placenta as well as in the first milk. It is, I am told, one of the obscure questions frequently asked at a veterinary finals *viva voce*. Without these antibodies, the puppy is in great danger from the organisms that normally plague canines. Puppies that are hand-reared and denied the protection afforded by this colostrum must certainly suffer from the fact that they have not ingested the first milk.

Within the first week of the Jack Russell terrier's life, he should be docked and have his dew claws removed. Docking is a barbarous custom, and many vets refuse to dock a puppy, stating, quite rightly, that it serves no useful purpose. In fact, cosmetic surgery seems to be under fire the world over at this moment. It is a survival of a series of dog tax laws, laws that made docked dogs exempt from tax. Curs were required to have their tails removed to prevent them harassing the deer in the Royal Forests and later to be exempt from tax. The verb to curtail is derived from this savage custom. At the time of writing, there are moves afoot to bring about legislation to outlaw docking, and though the Jack Russell terrier might look just a little strange with an undocked tail, I'm afraid in that event we'll have to get used to the sight. It is said the Reverend John Russell never docked his puppies and allowed them to sport natural squirrel tails, tails which were of use since he could grip the terrier by the stern and draw him from the earth. A terrier's tail should never be docked too short for this reason, and a bobtail terrier looks positively unsightly and badly balanced. Two thirds of the tail should be left when docking a terrier.

Docking may serve no useful purpose, but the removal of dew claws certainly does. Dew claws are small vestigial toes, sometimes found on the hind legs of puppies. If left uncut they snag in the long grass and cause the animal great distress. I have seen several bitches bleed copiously when their dew claws were caught up in brambles. There are some breeds where it is fashionable to leave the dew claws on. Pyrenean mountain dogs always have their dew claws left intact, as there is legend that it helps the dogs to climb rocks. Legend it is, however, with absolutely no basis in scientific fact, and a curious legend at that. Dan Russell, in his excellent book, *Jack Russell and His*

Terriers – a must for any student of cynology or West Country history – states that he does not remove dew claws on account of the fact that he believes they are of use when the dog is grooming himself. While I value the wisdom of the old master, and wisdom his advice invariably is, I cannot agree with him here. Dew claws are vestigial limbs, they are claws in a state of atrophy, a state of disuse, and as such serve no useful purpose. I always remove dew claws. Cobby had a saying about docking, wise as were all his sayings. He believed that if a litter was puny they should be docked at two days old, when there would be little blood in the caudal muscle. This docking would therefore not check the puppy as much as it would if it were done during the tenth day of its life. Cobby left strong, healthy puppies till they were a week old before docking them. Personally, I dock as early as possible. Two-day-old puppies are not too young to be docked.

The puppies begin to grow. Apart from the fact that a heavy vaginal discharge may continue for some time from the bitch, there will probably be little to concern the breeder. But it is no time to neglect the bitch and her brood, for, at the risk of a cliché, the breeder is not out of the wood yet. If the bitch is to rear her litter well she must be fed almost *ad lib* now, in contrast with the diet advised during pregnancy. The litter will certainly benefit from the dam's increased diet. At ten days old, the puppies will begin to open their eyes, and at fourteen days old, they may begin to suck scraped meat: finely macerated flesh, made by scraping a knife across raw and bloody meat. This is meat without fibre, and easily digested. Puppies whose dams are lactating heavily may refuse such meat at first, but an undernourished litter will certainly take the meat readily at a fortnight old.

With luck from here on it should be plain sailing and the breeder will soon be in a position to put his 'puppies for sale' advertisement in the paper. But, and this again is a big but, there are still maladies that can trouble the well-fed bitch and her litter. Often when a bitch is lactating heavily she will begin to totter, to walk with a stiff gait. If not treated immediately, she will pass rapidly into the most savage fit imaginable, the cause of her frightening ailment being hypocalcaemia. When a bitch lactates, various salts such as calcium salts are leached from her body to enrich the milk. To put it very simply, if these salts are not replenished rapidly, the brain 'misfires' and the bitch begins to thrash about with uncontrolled movements. Before the condition was properly understood, cure was impossible. Old veterinary surgeons called the complaint eclampsia, believing it to be the canine equivalent of human eclampsia, from the Latin *eclampo* – 'I explode'. This was subsequently proved not to be the case.

Milk fever or hypocalcaemia can easily be treated by a veterinary surgeon by injecting the bitch with a chemical called calcium boroglutinate, and recovery is often startlingly rapid. This injection is made into the raised vein of the foreleg, and I have seen bitches come out of a very bad fit so rapidly that they have savaged the needle before it could be withdrawn from the vein. Once a bitch has had a hypocalcaemic fit, it is advisable, or virtually essential, to wean the puppies and keep the bitch well away from her brood. I have seen bitches get a succession of these fits, and they needed a very large quantity of calcium boroglutinate to get them out of the thrashing convulsions later in the lactation. Success is not always so instantaneous or so certain, however. My best bitch died in a hypocalcaemic fit, failing to make the count when the vet injected enough calcium boroglutinate to ensure a Dane would recover. Cows with a high lactation level are frequent sufferers from this malady, but relatively little research has been done into the problem in dogs and cats.

From the evience I have gathered, and gathered in deadly earnest, I must add, for this complaint once nearly pushed my strain into extinction, certain conditions can bring on hypocalcaemia.

1. Bitches usually suffer from the malady between the seventh and twenty-third day of lactation. I have never found a bitch experiencing the problem under seven days or over twenty-three days after the birth of their puppies.
2. Bitches that are fed on a calcium-rich diet – synthetic calcium salts, such as calcium oleate and calcium lactate during pregnancy, often appear more susceptible to the complaint, and not less susceptible, as might be imagined.
3. Small dogs are more frequent sufferers than large dogs, particularly small dogs with large litters.
4. Second and third whelpers are more prone to this malady than first-time whelpers, probably because mature bitches give more milk.
5. Certain strains of terrier are more prone to hypocalcaemia than others. My own strain was particularly prone to milk fever.
6. Bitches that are well-fed, healthy and in good coat are more likely to go down with milk fever than emaciated bitches, possibly because well-fed, fat bitches lactate more heavily.

Hypocalcaemia is really a problem if the strain of dog being bred is prone to this disease. If it occurs very frequently, it is time to outcross to another blood line, that may be less prolific, perhaps, but which may not lactate as heavily and so not be as prone to the trouble.

My own strain was once rotten with the ailment, and, as I say, almost pushed into extinction. The problem was aggravated by my programme of in-breeding to the Seale Cottage strain, and to Pickaxe, the famous stud dog owned by John Cobby. Eventually I was forced to bring in an outcrop, a stud dog from the Chittingfold and Leconfield Hunt, a dog sired by Goddard's famous stud dog, Scrap. I lost just a little nose from the outcross, but gained some straightness of leg, mind you. My problem of milk fever in bitches, however, came to an abrupt end. Of course, not all terrier bitches are prone to the trouble, but it is wise to watch for symptoms as failure to do so can result in a dead bitch, for many hypocalcaemic fits lead to death if not treated promptly.

By three weeks old, even the best-fed puppies will begin to suck at meat and the bitch should be taken out to allow the puppies to feed. Many bitches vomit meat and meal for the puppies to eat. It is a bit revolting to look at, but simply nature's way of providing easily digested food for the babes to consume. Foxes, wolves and some wild dogs gorge at a kill and then fetch back the food for the cubs. Some bitches become frantic if denied the right to perform this age-old ritual. Bill Brockley of Etwall once had a bitch called Teazle, an archetypal earth-mother type of bitch who continued to vomit food for her four-month-old litter. Normally, by the time puppies are six weeks old, few bitches will perform this feat.

Whelps should be wormed before they are sold, for not only does the roundworm have a debilitating effect on the puppy, but worms are transferable to humans, and children particularly can become quite ill as a result of a disease called visceral larval migrans that is caused by the roundworm. I always seem to feel a little nauseated when I see chocolate box photographs of little girls holding up puppies to their faces – usually puppies that are less than three weeks old. Highly photogenic, perhaps, but also highly infectious. Puppies should be wormed at six weeks of age, and again at eight weeks before they are sold. Two wormings are usually enough to clear out a puppy. I use a liquid worming medicine called Erliworm made by Shaws, and this can be given to a puppy at three weeks old without any ill-effect. Two wormings are essential, usually at a fortnightly interval, since some of the eggs will survive the first worming and these will reinfect the puppy.

Puppies should be feeding well before they are sold. It is madness to sell a babe who is unweaned, since not only does the puppy suffer greatly, but the breeder gets a very bad name for sharp practice. A dead puppy is the only possible outcome of selling whelps that are unweaned. I believe that the authorities frown on the sale of six-week-old puppies and it is usually better to run one's babes until they are eight weeks old to ensure that the weaning process is complete.

At the time of writing, it is relatively easy to sell Jack Russell terriers, for they are small and, as they are unrecognized by the Kennel Club, are still very reasonably priced. If one shows regularly, one gains a reputation for having a reliable working strain. Puppies will usually go fairly rapidly without any more than verbal advertising. Dealers will usually take any surplus stock – at a reduced rate, of course. I dislike selling to dealers, not because of the supposedly massive profits they are reputed to make, but quite simply because I like to know to whom my puppies are being sold. A good home should be the first priority a breeder should consider, and a good home is not always the most prosperous home, I assure you.

Try to ensure that the temperament of the puppy suits that of the buyer. A boisterous little villain will certainly not suit an old lady. A sloppy sycophantic puppy will do badly with a man who has a few terriers already and who will be unable to give the sycophant the attention it deserves. Choose your clients carefully, and do not sell to obvious undesirables. Eventually, one gets to know the various types of would-be buyer to avoid. Avoid the type who doesn't believe in inoculating the puppy. This is a sure way of sentencing your pup to death. Likewise avoid the chap who tries to bid you down, to make you accept a lower price – for instance, if you ask him £20, he immediately offers you £15. He will usually be equally tight fisted about providing good food for the puppy, and he'll be a bit thrifty about inoculating as well. Above all, for God's sake, avoid selling a puppy to a customer who has recently lost a dog to some mysterious illness. Don't even allow him near your premises. It is a fair chance that the illness is either distemper or hepatitis – both diseases that would, in fact, spell certain death to the puppy you sell him and to all your stock as well. Try not to sell any terrier to a neurotic (my mother was one such), for these people are sheer hell on any animal, and, from my own experience, on kids as well, and the poor beast will live a life of absolute misery, becoming the whipping boy of the woman's own anxieties. Terriers are simply not suited to such a person, and such people would be better off with a Shetland sheepdog or a sedate spaniel, or, better still, no dog at all.

Turn away undesirable clients, for if you have good stock you will certainly sell your puppies, and need have no worries about that. Simply tell the undesirable client that the puppy is booked, or raise the price ridiculously to a point well beyond his pocket. You will be forgiven a white lie or so, I'm sure. Anyway, it is false economy to sell a puppy to unsuitable folk. Within a week they will be knocking on your door for their money back with a sick, bewildered or barmy puppy, mentally damaged by insensitive behaviour. Believe me, I've learnt that this can be so through bitter experience. Breed and rear good-quality stock, and you can choose your clients. Newspapers will bring a host of odd and fascinating people to your door. I've made several friends this way, and met quite a few rogues, too, as well as a goodly sprinkling of absolute lunatics. Incidentally, expect late-night phone calls from worried families who have just purchased a puppy and who are at a loss to know how to quieten a homesick dog. Such phone calls are usually a sign that the babe has gone to a good home – a good and caring home, that is. You will meet some really odd people though through an advertisement, and in time you will learn to recognize and reject the oddities and select the desirable customers. But the best of luck with your advertisement.

8 INBREEDING AND OUTCROSSING

No account of breeding would be complete without a reference to inbreeding and outcrossing, though of necessity it has to be a brief reference in a book of this size and type.

Inbreeding

This is basically the mating of related stock together. If the stock is not particularly closely related, such as the mating of grandson to granddaughter, then this diluted inbreeding is referred to as line breeding. It was a standard joke at one time that, if one's breeding experiments were a success, then it was called line breeding, but that if the same breeding experiments were failures, then one could blame it on inbreeding. Contrary to popular belief, inbreeding does not necessarily produce lunacy and constitutional weakness, though injudicious practice might well do so. Sufficient to say, Cleopatra was the result of three hundred years of brother-to-sister pairings and all racehorses were bred from three sires. Yet, unless one is very careful and knowledgable, inbreeding can cause problems. To see why, let us examine a typical set of breeding experiments and see the problems that can befall a would-be inbreeder out to create a strain; and, frankly, inbreeding is the only way to create a strain.

In one particular district there is a particularly good sire who, in addition to having excellent type, is a superb worker. Thus, not only are bitches brought to him, but the would-be creator of a strain decides to mate the stud to the best of the stud's own daughters. More than likely, the inbred litter will be sound in wind and limb, not in any way deranged and probably of excellent type, but this will not always be the case. My own breeding experiments, my own list of errors and deformities, may be useful to illustrate a point.

About ten years ago, I bred an excellent stud dog called Rupert by mating a daughter of Joan Begbie's bitch Seale Cottage Saucy to Charlie Lewis's famous champion Micky. Rupert was just about everything I wanted. He was neat, tiny and plucky, and had an excellent nose. Furthermore, he invariably stamped his own type. He

An even, level litter: the hallmark of the true-breeding strain.

was what is called a homozygous stud – a rare enough quality in Russells today, and very rare then. Although he was physically sound, he carried genes of two deadly deformities, the first one being called cleft palate (meaning no roof to the mouth), which prevents puppies from suckling, and thus any puppy affected dies a death from starvation up to a week after its birth, and a lingering, dehydrating death at that. Many supposedly fading puppies (a malady which might or might not also be caused by some viral hepatitis) from inbred families may quite simply be victims of cleft palates. The second genetic defect was hydrocephally, or water on the brain, a singularly unpleasant disorder that manifests itself at four or five weeks when the craniums develop a ridiculously enlarged dome shape reminiscent of the rivals of Dan Dare (which dates me a bit). Sadly, such a deformity is not indicative of a super IQ. It is quite simply a deformity that causes loss of balance, blindness and ultimately death.

Now, there was no way of telling which of Rupert's daughters and sons carried these hidden (recessive) faults except by breeding from them and mating them to a dog that carried the same defects. For example, from Rupert I bred a super rough-coated bitch called Troy and a nice, neat little smooth dog called Twirl. Both were of good physical type without obvious defects, but both, unknown to me at the time, carried cleft palate. A simple diagram will demonstrate what happened when they were mated (Figure 1).

Figure 1.

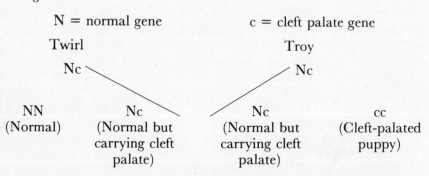

Thus one in every four puppies which Troy bred when mated to her half-brother would be cleft-palated, and as cleft-palated puppies cannot suckle, they simply die. In the first, and, I may add, only mating of this pair, the dice fell somewhat differently. I lost the entire batch of six puppies through cleft palate, each and every one possessing the abnormality. It took me nearly a year to trace back the defect to its source and eradicate the carriers of these vicious deformities, and I had many puppies born with lethal peculiarities during this testing period. There was no way of rectifying the problems within the strain. It could have been done, perhaps, but it would have taken twenty to thirty generations, and I should have bred a large number of deformed puppies during that time. My solution was to bring in an outcross puppy to use at stud, and I have never experienced the problem since. Yet, as I am still inbreeding my strain, I now get putty noses and bad shoulders when I inbreed to particular sires. Inbreeding is thwart with problems and dangers, and unless one knows exactly what one is doing and is prepared to cull ruthlessly, the mating of close relatives together always carries dangers. Here are a few principles about inbreeding:

1. Good qualities as well as bad are accentuated. In other words, by using a superb stud, the majority of his inbred puppies (inbred to that stud, that is) could also be quite classy.
2. As soon as abnormalities manifest themselves, it is time to go for a mating from another family of Jack Russells.
3. As one continues to inbreed, the percentage of deformities diminishes. This is a scientific fact, not a hypothesis, but the initial losses can be quite devastating.
4. Inbred stock is not automatically weaker than mongrel stock. Greyhounds are excellent examples of the truth of this statement. Most Waterloo Cup winners and White City champions are usually fairly closely related. Many are very inbred to certain noted sires, such as Hi There, who features in most present-day pedigrees. Yet, by dint of judicious inbreeding, the times recorded at greyhound tracks and trials are improving yearly. The operative phrase is 'judicious inbreeding', for the progeny are tested in the rigorous field of either coursing or the race track, the weak and inferior quickly going to the wall and only the strong and fit being allowed to survive. Such judicious inbreeding has produced the great athletic dog of today.

Outcrossing as a Way of Improving the Jack Russell Terrier

This is a subject of which most Jack Russell Club members fight shy, and I simply don't know why. There is a move afoot not to pass any dogs with obvious foreign blood for the Advanced Register in an effort to stop the outcrossing of Russells with other breeds of terrier to improve the shoulders, height, coat and so forth of the present Jack Russell terrier, the standard of most Jack Russell terriers being quite lamentably low at the time of writing. To be brutally frank, many

Jack Russell strains could well benefit from using the blood of other breeds – breeds which have had considerable time to have various congenital defects weeded out, the same defects which so beset the present-day Jack Russell terrier. Smooth fox terriers are commonly mated to Jack Russell terriers, and the progeny are usually very typy indeed. Most northern working terrier show winners have a liberal amount of fox terrier blood in their veins and are probably no worse for this foreign blood. John Winch, an expert on terrier conformation, once caused a minor storm at the Jack Russell Club Show in Llangollen by making a nearly pure fox terrier with only a dash of Jack Russell blood a champion. It provoked much criticism, but the dog certainly conformed to the standard laid down by the Jack Russell Club of Great Britain, and I for one could not fault Winch's decision.

Several excellent rough-coated terriers have been bred by crossing quite indifferent Jack Russell terriers with Lakeland or Border terriers. The first generation of this outcross are usually coloured, but if one of two courses is followed, a percentage of excellent rough-coated Jack Russell terrier types are produced (Figure 2).

Figure 2.

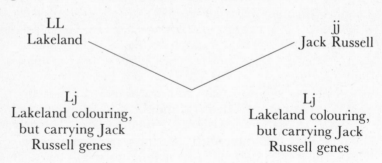

These siblings mated together would give:

Derek Hume of Consett produced some excellent rough-coated Russells by using this method of improvement, and his dogs also

Sparrow suggests that a bull terrier cross should be used periodically to improve head size.

work for the Braes of Derwent Hunt, so criticism about ruining the working quality of the breed by outcrossing is not only ill-founded but also ridiculous. If Hume had used poodle blood to improve his type, then complaint would have been valid, for it would have ruined the true terrier nature of the progeny. As it was, he used the very best Fell terriers available, and his stock have certainly stood up to any attack concerning their working ability.

My own strain of Jack Russell was suffering from fairly weak snipy jaws when I outcrossed to some really tough bull terrier-headed brown terriers, erroneously known as Patterdales. These terriers were bred by Bray of Kirby Lonsdale in Lancashire, and his strain bred true to type. My first generation was therefore all brown, but my second generation produced the grandmother of my dog Vampire and the heads improved accordingly. Until the Jack Russell terrier has been standardized and improved a great deal in type, such judicious crossing can only have a beneficial effect, regardless of the enraged comments of purists.

Curiously the British, the most mongrelly of races, are the very worst snobs regarding racial purity of stock. Once more, may I resort to the greyhound to show how carefully planned outcrossing has no deleterious effect. Lord Orford, the father of competitive coursing, used very game bulldogs to cross with his greyhounds to produce the gutsy dogs required for coursing. All modern greyhounds have this bulldog blood, and the breed is not a whit inferior for such an introduction. The madness to preserve racial purity of a mongrelly type like that of the Jack Russell terrier is ludicrous to say the least.

Border terrier blood is often used to produce good, narrow, rough terriers here in the Midlands, and some very good-quality dogs have been produced by using a son of the famous Maxton Matchless. Again, the first generation are brown, or blue and tan, but the second generation produces a quarter of the litter coloured like Jack Russell terriers, and only the otter head of the progeny gives any indication that foreign blood has been used in the production of these good-coated rough dogs. I hasten to add that this is usually a good, strong head, well suited to the working dog produced. As I have said, however, the practice is contested by the purists of the Jack Russell Terrier Club. Sufficient only to add that it is a method of stock improvement which is, at the time of writing, frequently used. I shall await with fascination the storm of protests which this section will arouse as soon as the book is published.

The Dog Breeders Act

This was an Act that was passed in 1973 to alleviate the lot of dogs bred in the dog factories of the 1960s, and, believe me, some of those dog factories were pretty terrible places, places that would make Dickensian squalor look particularly palatial. The Act was designed to ensure that such breeding dogs were at least given a reasonable diet, a chance to exercise and an opportunity to rear their numerous litters in some degree of comfort. Like most Acts regarding the keeping of livestock, it simply hasn't worked in a majority of boroughs in the country. Some dreadful breeding kennels, licensed and unlicensed, still exist in certain places, and some public health officials obviously seem to regard the Act as a joke – an attitude that should merit prosecution of those officials, in my own opinion, for they have quite openly flouted the statute passed by the government. Dreadful hell-holes masquerading as breeding kennels still exist, and although a few are exposed by the national press from time to time, usually during a week when news is in short supply, far more pass unnoticed.

When the Act was first passed, the public health authorities were at a bit of a loss as to how to implement it, but, by now, fairly clear-cut rules must exist about the minimum conditions that should be allowed in breeding kennels. It is a tragedy that the public health authorities should be so lax about enforcing the Act. Briefly, the Act provides that:

1. Any person with two or more breeding bitches, bitches used to produce puppies for sale, must register his or her premises with the local council. If one does not intend to breed from one's bitches, there is no need to register the premises. Failure to register one's premises can result in fines of up to £200. At the outset there were some prosecutions of offenders who had failed to register their premises, but now such prosecutions are rare, either because the public have become more law-abiding, or, more likely, because local councils have not the facilities to implement the Dog Breeders Act.
2. The Act states that dogs should be kept in buildings with non-absorbant walls, either brick, concrete or wooden kennels that have been lined with either metal or a fibreglass type of plastic. This is to facilitate easy cleaning and to prevent, or at least reduce, the transference of diseases such as mange and leptospirosis.
3. Dogs should have access to impervious runs. In other words, earth runs must be concreted or bricked. This is again meant to facilitate easy cleaning of the runs and to prevent the spread of infections. Earth runs are usually disease-filled, anyway, for tape-worm eggs will live in such conditions for a decade or so.
4. Heating of some form must be provided for puppy rearing. This heating can be by electrical heat lamps or any other method, but a fire extinguisher must be kept close at hand in case a fire breaks out in the kennels.
5. A public health official must be allowed access to the premises at any time to ensure these regulations are being fulfilled, also that dog food is being kept in conditions unlikely to encourage vermin; that is, in rat-proof bins and so on.

To being with, I considered the Act to be an imposition or restriction on human liberty, but, on reflection, it is not. It is an Act designed to ensure that no bitch should live out her life in absolute misery, producing puppy after puppy in filth and disease. In fact it is an excellent, well-thought-out Act of Parliament. The damnable pity of it is that it is so rarely implemented.

9 WORKING TERRIER SHOWS

If you are able to laugh at defeat, take apparently insane decisions as a joke, tolerate obvious injustice with a smile, behave like the paragon in Kipling's 'If', the terrier shows are indeed good fun. If, however, you need to win the coveted rosette valued 10p, think your terrier is without fault, a flawless and perfect animal, are unable to suffer fools gladly, become bitter or enraged by huntsmen and masters placing obviously monstrous dogs above yours, then I suggest you give terrier showing a wide berth – and a very wide berth, at that. Terrier shows are, for the most part, staged as social events, more as get-togethers than make-or-break tests and, reasons for living. They should be regarded as places to meet and make friends, good fun and nothing more. Sadly, they are taken all too seriously, and that is where the trouble really starts and the fur, both canine and human, begins to fly.

Basically, there are three types of working terrier show:

1. Shows staged by hunt gymkhanas and country fairs to attract a crowd and finance some event – either a hunt event or, in most cases, a very deserving charity.
2. Shows staged by the Fell and Moorland Club, a club that specializes in rescuing trapped terriers and usually runs very well-organized shows for working terrier men, catering for all breeds of terriers suitable for working fox and badger. Breeds such as Borders, Lakelands and what is erroneously called the Patterdale are found here, as well as Jack Russell terriers. The funds raised by such a show are usually used to provide money to rescue trapped terriers, pay for hire of excavators and so on.
3. The shows staged by the Jack Russell Terrier Club of Great Britain, and these are the only shows exclusively for Jack Russell terriers. These lump together with the sundry other Jack Russell clubs, some of the founders of whom were banished from the original club for obstructive behaviour or other minor peccadilloes.

Hunt terrier shows come in for a fair amount of criticism, justly so, perhaps, since the judges are simply huntsmen or masters who have been invited along to judge simply to create good relationships between the hunts. Few pretend to be experts on terriers, and most admit to not knowing one end of a terrier from another. Should the reader wish to attend such a show, remember that if you pay a fee to enter a class, your fee is simply your way of asking a judge for his opinion of your dog. If it is not also an opinion which you share, then that's too bad. Grin and bear it, or, better still, don't attend the shows in the first place. Most huntsmen have curious views about what constitutes the ideal working terrier, and some strange dogs gain the coveted rosettes.

Sometimes, in desperation, and to give the show results a more authentic ring, a vet may also be invited to judge. While these gentlemen can pick out such defects as patella luxation (hip displacia) among others, it would be insane to think that they were necessarily qualified to give an opinion on any dog that it is being bred to a standard. Most hunt shows are fairly casual, both in entry regulations and efficiency, but most of all in judging. They are worth going to see, if only to get some idea of the social life and *bonhomie* associated with the hunting, shooting, fishing set, but also, I am afraid, to watch the antics, tantrums and sheer bad sportsmanship of some of the exhibitors. At one show I attended I was amazed to see an irate little man hurling over the display table in rage at not being placed in the under 10-inch class of terrier, a class that, I must admit, was won by a 12-inch terrier dog, but there it is, at a hunt show anything still goes, I'm afraid. Even so, I really enjoy hunt terrier shows. There is such a variety of really pleasant people present, and most hunt shows are fairly lout free. Apart from the enraged lunatics and bad losers, a hunt terrier show can make a very pleasant day out for the family.

Any terrier may enter in such shows, though it would be fair to mention that as a rule the winners will be either Jack Russell terriers or Lakelands or Border terriers, or crosses between the said breeds. Again, I repeat, do not expect the organization or judging ability found at Crufts. Most judges of hunt shows are not only recognizable by their judging rosettes and bowler hats, but also by their somewhat embarrassed expressions at being asked to officiate at all. Most will quite openly admit that terriers are simply not their scene.

Club shows are rather a different matter. They include the now almost minute Midland Working Terrier Club and the very large and thriving Fell and Moorland Working Terrier Club. These clubs also cater for a variety of terriers suitable for working fox and badger, but it is rare to find Kennel Club registered breeds at such shows, other than Border terriers and the odd Lakeland terrier. These shows are usually judged by working terrier breeders, and though they are organized by club officials for the purpose of raising funds to rescue trapped terriers, the results are often regarded with deadly seriousness by the competitors. There are usually a large number of exhibits at these shows, which are, incidentally, highly well-organized indeed, and classes for lurchers are also staged in conjunction with the terrier show, disastrous fights sometimes resulting from the mixture of the rather phlegmatic long dog and the aggressive terrier. Jack Russells of a very high standard may sometimes be found at these shows.

Lastly we come to shows staged by the Jack Russell Club of Great Britain. At the time of writing, such shows are usually given a fairly clear berth by most working terrier men, though why this should be so is difficult to say. Perhaps it is something to do with the last bastion of male chauvinism, for such meets are usually organized by women. The shows are usually reasonably well run, and though it has been the practice to employ Kennel Club judges with no knowledge of working terriers, some of the decisions made by these judges do reach a fairly high standard. This fact is hotly disputed by many terrier men, who believe that a man must work his terriers to understand conformation – a belief that somewhat defies logic.

The classes for dogs of the Advanced Register standard are, at the time of writing, quite lamentable, and many of the exhibits are of very poor quality indeed – a fact that has been the reason for many members refusing to have their dogs listed on the Advanced Register. Perhaps the club has set its sights far too low, or maybe it is expedient to pass dogs for the register for the sake of maintaining goodwill and keeping high membership. It is difficult to say. Sufficient to say that at one show in South Wales, the standard of the Advanced Register exhibits was so low that the crowd of spectators passed comments about it being 'a comic dog class'. Perhaps time will improve this lamentably low standard of stock, but, for the present, if the future of the Jack Russell is being determined by these exhibits, then the possibilities of breed improvement look bleak indeed.

Classes for working certificated dogs are staged at all these shows, and are usually fairly badly attended. This is not because there are few Jack Russell terriers worked, but simply because few owners bother to obtain Hunt Working Certificates. Working certificates which state that such and such a dog has worked with a hunt and has proved game are of mixed value. Some hunts, the Atherstone, for example, print quite lavish certificates, while others merely issue scraps of paper. Many working terrier men scoff at these certificates, stating that they are not worth the paper they are written on, and maybe, in some cases, it is true. Certainly some working certificates are granted to dogs who have not seen much work to fox or badger. On the whole, however, this isn't true. I have collected seventy-five working certificates with various hunts, and each and every one of these dogs were worked regularly to fox; and while it is true to say that most terriers will work if given a chance, it is also fair to add that the working certificated classes do at least try to ensure that the working instinct is kept alive in the Jack Russell terrier.

If one shows regularly and is reasonably successful, then, sooner or later, the terrier exhibitor will be asked to judge. Make no mistake about it, terrier judging is both traumatic and tiring, for shows often go on for a full four or five hours. Furthermore, it is wise to remember that the scathing comments you formerly heard at the edge of the ring when you were a spectator will be said about you now that you are a judge. Therefore it is only good sense to make a reasonable and fair show at the job. You cannot please all of the people, and a good many people believe that their dog is unbeatable and become very irritable with your decisions, but a quiet, efficient manner will often pay. These few points will help to make your first judging engagement go a little more smoothly than it otherwise might:

1. For heaven's sake, get to know the standard of the breed you are to judge and stick to it. If you are questioned as to your decision, you can then quote the standard and perhaps skate out of trouble.
2. Avoid personal preferences. For example, 'That old dog looks a bit like our so and so and he was a good 'un, a grand worker even though he was ugly as hell, so I'll put the old dog first' – a disastrous mistake, believe me.
3. Don't be afraid to put up a classy terrier who has never seen work. The prizes are for the most suitable terrier to work, not for the dog with the most wounds. Dogs sans teeth, sans eyes, sans ears, sans all, have more than likely had another dog behind them pushing them into the quarry. Hence wounds count for nothing when assessing a terrier as the most suitable working dog; or dog to work, would be more accurate.
4. Don't invite friends to show under you. This is sheer madness. If you give one a prize the rest of the class will criticize you. If you don't give one a prize, you will lose a friend. I always beg my associates to stay away when I am judging. Inviting friends will certainly cause bad feeling. I showed at Preston once, and exhibited a super little dog who won a great number of prizes. I was placed fifth in a class of five in this show behind two with bad mouths and one with crooked legs. The judge placed the winners with comments like, 'You here, Alf'; 'You second here, Ted.' I take my defeats graciously, at least I hope I do, but I have to confess that I was just a little bitter on that occasion. Friends exhibiting under you don't help your image at shows, believe me.

5. Never be influenced by pre-show chat designed to make you put up a particular dog, nor should you be influenced by comments made in the ring. Baffled, reader? Let me explain, for it will certainly happen. You are standing next to a tent with a rosette proclaiming to all the world that you are a judge. Man with dog on lead stands next to you, shouting to no one in particular, 'Won it again last week, Ginger, good judge that.' This is to make you think that if you, too, put up the said dog, you, too, will be labelled 'a good judge'. It is a most common pre-show trick. In the ring, tricks are equally common. You pass near an obviously experienced exhibitor with an unwholesome desire to win (and, believe me, the desire to win is near mania with some exhibitors), but you do not place his dog. You stop at a nice tricolour and examine it. 'He doesn't work it,' shouts the experienced exhibitor. So what? It shouldn't influence your decision one iota. Another grand con trick is performed by the man with a dog with a crooked mouth. You reach down to examine the said dog. 'For God's sake watch him, he'll have your hand off,' and the exhibitor shows you the corner of the dog's mouth. First rule, if you can't examine a dog properly because it is savage, *then don't place it*. One famous exhibitor won forty-odd shows with a dog with a crooked mouth, a dog, I might add, who on account of his wins mated numerous bitches and produced dozens of dogs with crooked mouths. There are many tricks to showing, but try to resist any browbeating, bullying, sales talk and even bribes, and believe it or not I have been offered bribes to give an exhibitor a tenpenny rosette.

Remember, you are doing the judging. It is your decision. And the best of luck with your first judging engagement. It is literally a terrifying experience.

10   AILMENTS AND DISEASES

It is said that the Jack Russell terrier is relatively disease free, but this is certainly a moot point. While it is, more often than not, free from the genetic deformities that so beset some of the Kennel Club registered breeds of terrier, this is simply because the breed is not particularly profitable to produce and thus commercial breeders tend to stay clear of this type of dog. Hence the breed has been in the hands of small-time breeders and working terrier men, and because of this it seems probable that the weakly and the deformed have perhaps gone to the wall. The strong and the fit have certainly survived. Disease free the breed is not, however, for any working terrier is likely to come into contact with foxes, or at least rats, and these alone are very, very fruitful sources of infections of every kind. Any terrier man worth his salt should therefore know the various canine diseases that can infect his dog, for not only can these diseases harm his dog, but many of these infections are communicable from dogs to human beings.

First and foremost, it would be wise to deal with the more lethal infections, that for reasons that will be obvious later, I will group together as the Big Four. Not only are these the most deadly, dangerous infections, but they can also be so easily prevented by inoculating the dog.

Distemper

This is really the result of a group of viruses, all of which cause similar symptoms and all of which have one thing in common: they cause severe illness and frequently death. As I have stated, the disease is caused by a very tiny virus, and since viruses are totally immune to the counter-onslaught of antibiotics, there is very little one can do to treat the disease once it becomes firmly established. The patent medicine called Lucanis, recommended by Sir Jocelyn Lucas in his book *The Working Terrier*, has just about the same effect as antibiotics. Lucas was no fraud, but he wrote his epic in 1930 before virology was understood and well before Fleming opened the door to antibiotics.

Many old terrier books suggest that if a dog wears a collar treated with Stockholm tar, it becomes immune to the ravages of distemper, and many breeders have allowed their dogs to wear such a collar in the mistaken idea that it would keep the disease at bay. Sadly, this is another ridiculous untruth, an example of clutching at a straw in the forlorn hope that one's beloved pet will not fall prey to distemper, or quite simply of ignorance as to the cause of the disease. In pre-inoculation days, the fact that a dog had survived distemper increased its sales value three- or four-fold, and a newspaper in my possession, dated the same year as Rawden Lee wrote *The Fox Terrier*, has an advertisement for a dog which reads 'Over Distemper' as an appraisal of the dog's qualities. Before the days of inoculation against distemper, the pet owner lived in constant dread of his dog contracting this killing disease. Distemper occurs in waves, the disease thinning the dog population in a district like a winnowing wind, reducing the canine population dramatically and filling the animal shelters with pitiful, hopeless cases. It is a very distressing disease, made all the more distressing because it is today totally unnecessary for a dog to suffer from its effects.

Distemper manifests itself insidiously. One day the dog may be hale and hearty, the next day slightly off colour and the third day decidedly ill. Usually the first concrete symptoms that the dog is infected with distemper and not simply off colour is the fact that the eyes become gummed up with a particularly nasty pus, a pus that is corrosive enough to remove the fur from around the eyes, giving the dog an almost ghostly, spectral appearance. The normal temperature of a healthy dog is 101.5 °F, but distemper will send this temperature soaring, though in some cases the disease may cause the temperature to drop well below 101.5 °F. Distemper takes about three weeks to run its course, and the effects frequently include death, or, more sickeningly still, paralysis. The disease is all the more terrifying because, quite frequently, the patient appears to recover and lose the pitiful far-away look of the sufferer, all appearing to be well again, when quite suddenly it goes into a severe thrashing fit. This is usually the precursor of even more terrifying fits, and paralysis of the limbs is often an aftermath of the convulsions. In 1974, the disease hit my kennels when I had 'in training' two Border terrier puppies too young to inoculate. Both contracted distemper and both were very seriously ill. Fortunately (though, in the light of experience, was it fortunate?) the puppies were well looked after by two twelve-year-old girls who worked part-time with my terriers. These two youngsters, one of whom is now a trainee vet, kept the puppies warm and kept a day-and-night watch over their wards. Miraculously the puppies began to recover, and were just about to be returned to my kennels from the houses of the young girls when one puppy developed a pronounced tic.

Within hours, both puppies were in the throes of thrashing fits, one dying that night and the second spending three more days of struggle before the child would let me put the puppy down. It is an experience I shall never forget.

Even if the infected dog recovers from the disease and escapes the devastating fits associated with the infection, there are other side-effects that are fairly unpleasant. Usually the teeth of an infected dog suffer quite badly, the enamel becoming pitted and thus decay of the teeth being greatly speeded up. Strangely, even in these supposedly enlightened times when dog owners are reputedly educated to the dangers of distemper, it is surprising how many dogs with distemper-damaged teeth may be found at the shows. Last year I judged a class of veteran terriers at a hunt show in the south of England and was confronted with four old war horses, three of which had teeth with the tell-tale distemper marks. True, they had recovered enough to live to a ripe old age, but how many puppies died during the out-breaks that infected these old warriors, and were they the sole survivors of whole litters, I wonder?

Old books describe distemper as a specific disease; specific, that is, to dogs, for it was hitherto thought to be a disease confined only to canines. Ike Matthews, an Edwardian rat catcher, was a bit quicker than the veterinary profession at noticing how, whenever the disease hit the working terrier man's kennels, a few days before the symptoms of the disease manifested themselves among the dogs, the ferrets which were part and parcel of most working terrier men's or rat catchers' establishments became infected with an incurable disease called 'sweats' and the ferrets promptly died. Long before veterinary research recognized that the sweats about which Matthews spoke and distemper of dogs were the same disease, rat hunters realized that an outbreak of distemper would see off both dogs and ferrets. Badgers, stoats, weasels and foxes also fall victim to these viruses, and in 1970 it was no uncommon occurrence to take infected foxes in the middle of Birmingham, for that was a year which saw a particularly virulent strain of distemper sweep the city.

On the subject of strains of virus, dog breeders of old knew quite a lot about the virulence of the disease. Vero Shaw stated in one article that there were some types of distemper that were less injurious than others. In this respect, he was quite right. In 1958, Laidlaw and Dunkin completed a masterly piece of work on the nature of the distemper strains. Briefly, they showed that three major types of distemper strain existed. Virus type A was a highly danger-ous strain, recorded by Laidlaw and Dunkin to be the original type of distemper that frequently killed its victims. Virus type B was a rare type of infection, not often encountered in Britain, while Virus C was a common type of disease that sometimes killed, but more often than not caused no more than a high temperature and a few days of lassitude.

However, Laidlaw and Dunkin's findings did not take into consideration the effect of any of these viruses in districts like Cumberland, where few working terriers are inoculated and the disease is rarely encountered owing to the relative isolation of the district – an isolation which, as I have incidentally explained in *The Working Terrier*, produced a variety of breeds of working dogs. Immunity to this disease must be practically nil in such districts, and an outbreak of even the mildest form of Virus C infection could have catastrophic effects on an uninoculated dog population. To the fool who states that working terriers in such districts are a tough race, as are the men and hounds of these bleak areas (probably a true enough statement, for most men, dogs and horses of these districts are noted for their constitutions), may I point out that in the early part of this century a mild form of distemper (believed by Collins to be a C type virus outbreak) infected the Greenland huskies and almost extinguished a whole breed of these, the world's most tough and constitutionally sound race of dogs.

Puppies are particularly prone to distemper, and the disease is frequently fatal when it infects uninoculated youngsters. When puppies are born, they have some immunity to this disease, an immunity being conferred by antibodies which pass via the placenta and also the colostrum, or first milk. Many books, and some veterinary books among them, state that this immunity lasts until the puppies are twelve weeks old and that by that age it is expedient to inoculate the puppy. Actually, antibody resistance to distemper becomes a little shaky, to say the least, after the second week of the puppy's life, as I found out to my cost in 1974.

In the January of that year, my crop of ferrets died very suddenly and in about a week my kennels of over a hundred working terriers were in the grip of one of the worst outbreaks of an A type virus distemper imaginable. At first I was upset about the loss of my ferrets, but not disturbed about the disease in my kennels as all my adult terriers were inoculated. I did, however, have numerous pregnant bitches on my premises, and I was about to learn a lot about antibody resistance to the disease the hard way – and a very costly lesson in biology it proved.

Logically speaking, my bitches should have been in contact with the virus, and as they had been inoculated against the virus, first, through the vaccine and secondly by contact with the real McCoy, they should have had a very high antibody level in their bodies, a level that should have passed on to the suckling puppies via the colostrum. So far, so good, but here theory ends and practice begins, and sadly there can often be a huge gap between the two. My puppies were born hale and hearty, but by three weeks of age whole litters had died. I was prepared to lose one or maybe two litters, and to write it off as simply bad luck, but litter after litter passed away and things became desperate. As a biologist, I took a long, scientific look at the situation and came up with absolutely nothing.

There were three courses of action open to me. First, no adult dog had died, so it was common sense to inoculate all pregnant bitches with distemper vaccine to boost their antibody levels still further, allowing it to pass on to the puppies through the colostrum. I did. It didn't work. To be honest, I didn't really expect it to. Next I decided to inoculate all the puppies with a measles vaccine as soon as they were three weeks old. Now, the measles virus is remarkably similar to the distemper virus, hence the theory that the cells of puppies will fill up with measles and reject the distemper virus. This is, of course, over-simplifying the facts, and this method also failed to work.

In sheer desperation, I was about to take the third option: not to breed any puppies for six months to allow the virus to die off. Then my vet brought in an expert from the Burroughs Wellcome laboratories. I thought I knew a great deal about distemper at this time, but my knowledge was put to shame by this quiet, self-effacing scientist. He suggested that I inoculate all my puppies at two weeks of age with a weakened strain of distemper, the sort used to inoculate all dogs. I did. My losses stopped abruptly. My place had become a grave-yard, with losses amounting to 107 puppies, but no inoculated adult dog experiencing any more than a slight attack of distemper; that is, runny eyes, high temperature and slight lassitude.

Obviously the only answer to distemper is to inoculate against the infection. This inoculation can be done as early as eight weeks, but most veterinary surgeons advise waiting until the puppy is twelve weeks old and the antibody level of the puppies is practically nil. Inoculation of healthy puppies, however, rarely ever checks the growth of these puppies, contrary to some amazingly illogical and unscientific articles that have appeared in the dog papers recently, though it is obvious madness to give an extra dose of distemper to an already infected puppy. Neither do I know of any cases where the inoculation actually started a distemper outbreak, so yet another fallacy has been debunked, I hope.

While inoculation is not one hundred per cent effective against distemper, it is fair to add that I have never known an inoculated adult become ill with distemper, even during the most severe outbreaks. Again, I repeat, inoculation is an essential. At the time of writing, there is a proposal that the dog licence fee should be increased to something like £5. Perhaps it would be a good idea to make the fee payable to a vet in exchange for inoculation, and then the additional revenue obtainable from the licence fees could be used for manufacturing distemper inoculants and, what is more important, to further distemper research so that the disease finally becomes extinct in Britain. It would be a mammoth task to make a disease extinct, but the diphtheria campaign proved that it could be done.

Hardpad should be included in any chapter on distemper, for hardpad is simply similar to a Virus A type of distemper. It first made its appearance in 1948, and was so destructive that many veterinary surgeons classed it as a separate disease. Paradistemper is now a more common name for this infection, and inoculation is, again, the answer. As a matter of interest, the disease was called hardpad because it causes the soles of a dog's feet to harden so that the animal often starts to clatter when it walks. The leather of the dog's nostrils also hardens. Again, I repeat, inoculation is a sure answer to this disease.

Should, even so, a dog contract distemper – and it must be stressed that, while very few inoculated dogs will be affected, most uninoculated dogs will almost certainly experience this disease – treatment is not only lengthy, costly and tedious, but also frequently most unsatisfactory. There is literally nothing one can give the dog to cure the infection. All you can hope to do is assist it to build up its constitution and so counteract the effects of the disease. The patient should be kept warm and made as comfortable as possible. The dog's eyes should be cleaned three or four times a day to prevent the accumulation of the caustic pus – pus which usually denudes the skin around the eyes of fur.

Lung infections frequently follow a debilitating attack of distemper, and these secondary infections, just like the sort of complaints that plague a human recovering from a serious illness, need expert medical treatment, possibly with antibiotics, if the dog is to be cured. Prior to the development of antibiotics, secondary lung infection was treated by allowing the patient to inhale Friars Balsam, though a more common remedy in my own district used to be to get the dog to inhale paraffin vapour. I have always considered this to be a somewhat dangerous old wives' remedy, but many of my neighbours swear by the treatment. I beg the reader, however, not to try these interesting old remedies.

Stomach upsets are also more than common and vomiting is almost an invariable extra of distemper. As a rule, traditional antacid chemicals will keep this in check, and bicarbonate of soda or chalk dust was used in old-fashioned hound kennels.

Convulsions, fits and chorea (St Vitus's Dance) are another matter. 'Time to go home,' as one of my veterinary friends says cynically, for reasons I shall now explain. Fits can be kept in check by injections or tablets of chemicals called anti-spasmodics, though, as a rule, they only curb and do not cure the malady. There is no cure for these disorders, and the paralysis which follows severe convulsions usually worsens as time goes on.

One story to alleviate the gloom of the last few paragraphs, however. Not all patients are crippled by these fits. One bitch I bred developed distemper at four months of age, and manifested no symptoms of any kind at all, though her litter mates died. She showed no sign of any of the distemper problems until she was sixteen months old, and then only after I mated her. After four weeks of pregnancy, she suffered a very bad fit, and for a while I suspected toxaemia. However, she whelped her litter normally and went on to become the great grandmother of my team of terriers. At the time of writing, she is eighteen, still hale and hearty. Hope, the dregs of Pandora's box, perhaps. Sufficient to say, the rest of the litter died. I am convinced they would have lived had they been inoculated.

Canine Viral Hepatitis, or Rubarth's Disease

More gloom here, I'm afraid, and gloom it is indeed, for this is a real killer. Whole kennels have passed away in days when this virus has struck, and it would be most interesting to have so and so's old Tip, or whatever his name might be, autopsied – old Tip, who was never ill, but who passed away in his sleep aged eight (a common enough occurrence amongst dogs that are uninoculated, I fear).

Some years ago I became absolutely fascinated with this infection and spent hours scraping lamp-posts against which dogs had urinated to extract the dried urine found on them. Once I was actually taken to a police station for my eccentricity, but fortunately the local constabulary have learned to live with my near-lunacy. I did learn, however, that there are few lamp-posts or such-like marking posts that are not riddled with the virus.

Of 106 posts I examined, only two proved hepatitis free, and those hepatitis-free samples were taken after a shower which could have washed the virus away. Dogs can pick up the disease simply by sniffing such locations, and once an uninoculated dog does so, then one could run a book that he will not recover. Normally, death occurs within forty-eight hours after the onset of the disease, and dogs that do survive the attack for five or six days will usually recover. Will Humphries, the famous setter breeder, and a wise, educated, articulate man at that, once told me that, next to distemper, this was the disease he feared most, and during the early part of this century, before the days of inoculation, he would allow no strange dog on his estate at Rattlinghope and Stretton-in-the-Dale.

Like distemper, viral hepatitis is a disease caused by a very tiny virus, so antibiotics have no effect on the progress of the infection, though they may certainly curb the secondary infections that race in to ail the infected dog. Usually the disease strikes so quickly that the layman is unable to recognize the symptoms until it is too late. Fever, dullness, extreme listlessness and keratitis, or 'blue eye', may manifest themselves within hours. Rapid wasting of the body becomes all too obvious, and is nearly always a sign that it is already too late to treat this killing disease. Some vets prescribe anti-serum and injections of vitamin K as a cure, but most veterinary surgeons are fairly honest about the fact that, once the disease has struck, there is little they can do except hope for the best.

A number of American hound kennels in pre-inoculation days were wiped out by the infection, and many wise hunters recommended that their establishments then be left fallow for years to allow the disease to clear, for the virus has a long life and dogs that have been infected can pass the disease in their urine for six or more months after recovery. Again, I stress, recovery is remarkably rare. Puppies can be inoculated against the disease at twelve weeks and the inoculation is usually one hundred per cent effective as a preventative measure.

Seldon, one of the earliest proprietors of boarding kennels in Britain, and certainly one of the most enlightened, believed that, prior to the Boarding Kennel Act, which insists on a fair degree of hygiene in boarding kennels, they were the greatest source of canine viral hepatitis. In fact, no reputable boarding kennel today will accept uninoculated dogs on their premises.

Leptospirosis

Now this is the disease that the rat hunter should really get to know, for rats are its most notorious carriers. Monlux, who researched the disease thoroughly in the United States during 1948, came up with some staggering figures about its nature and statistics. Fifty-five per cent of all the rats he investigated carried the disease, and 66.2 per cent of all city rats were regular death traps for any terrier keen enough to catch them. This disease, called by Ike Matthews 'rat catcher's yellows', was always the bane of rat-catching hunters, man and dog alike, for the disease can also be fatal to man, though in modern parlance it is in human medicine known as Weil's disease. Call it what you will, it can be lethal to dog and man alike. In fact, there are few creatures which it will not infect. Horses, cats, dogs, humans, pigs – name any animal and the disease can harm it. Only the rat, the most common carrier of this deadly bug, is seemingly unaffected by its ravages. There seems to be a strange irony here.

Ravages seems to be an appropriate word for the symptoms of the disease, for it affects the liver of the dog, which, next to the heart, is the most vital organ in the mammalian body. Any disorder of the liver causes the bile to be diverted from the gut, and since the bile colours the droppings of an animal, the faeces of the dog become putty-coloured, being devoid of the pigment passed on by the bile. This brown pigment, caused by the breakdown of blood corpuscles and other wastes, must go somewhere, however, and it is deposited around the body, in the skin, on the eyeballs, on the gums, on the tongue, on the soles of the feet. This is what gives rise to the second symptom of leptospirosis: namely, a yellowing of the tissues, otherwise known as jaundice, from the French *jaune* which means 'yellow'. At this stage, the dog is usually a bit off colour, listless, reluctant to keep up during walks, and though it is off its food and refusing the most tempting meats, shows a marked thirst – and for a damned good reason, for the body is desperately trying to wash out the filth that leptospirosis has produced. The droppings are extremely foetid as the function of the alimentary canal has gone awry, and in spite of the fact that copious amounts of water will be consumed, the animal becomes emaciated and very dehydrated. Kidney failure frequently follows, and death is usually the final result.

Treatment is a little tricky, to say the least, and consists of massive shots of a suitable antibiotic. Penicillin seems only to be moderately effective against this infection. And moderately is the operative word, I'm afraid, for infected animals frequently die. Furthermore, as I have said, it is highly contagious to humans. A macabre story will illustrate the dangers. In India, about ten years ago, a lay dentist felt a little off colour, and though he did not display the symptoms of the disease, nevertheless was found to be infected with leptospirosis. While making an injection of Novocaine or a similar pain killer, he had accidentally pricked his finger, and then injected a small child with the needle that had drawn blood from his own hand. A few days later, he displayed the symptoms of the disease, including jaundice, and in spite of intensive treatment died. The child also died six days later from the same disease. A dog or human does not even have to come into direct contact with a live rat to develop the disease. All a man needs to do is place a hand where a rat or infected dog has urinated, and the spirochaete can enter through any abrasion of the skin. Ten years ago, a council workman was cleaning a brook in Pelsall, Staffordshire, when he placed his hand near a rat warren. He died six days after the symptoms of leptospirosis manifested themselves. To take any sort of liberty with rats, simply to allow them on one's premises, is literally to dice with death.

During the nineteenth century, when the rat pits of London were so popular, Jimmy Shaw, a decayed pugilist, maintained an emporium where 2,000 rats were kept for testing the dogs of clients in the sickening arenas. He always obtained his rats from families who lived in the proximity of St Andrews Street, London. Towards the end of his life, Shaw lamented that he could no longer obtain his prizes from these families, for few had survived the highly profitable but dangerous years of live rat catching.

If the treatment is usually unsatisfactory, prevention of the disease is remarkably easy, cheap and effective. The puppy can be injected against it at twelve weeks old, and though the dog has to be reinoculated each year against leptospiral jaundice, prevention is nearly one hundred per cent effective. Perhaps inoculation may seem expensive to the average dog keeper, but it is only a fraction of the price a vet would charge to try and cure a dog of the disease. Leptospirosis, which was the scourge of kennels one hundred years ago, is now largely a thing of the past, thanks to the researches which have led to the inoculation of dogs against the infection.

Canicola Fever

At the risk of seeming to become a bore, this is yet another killer, and before the would-be dog keeper throws up his hands in horror at the dangers that can beset his dogs, forsaking them to keep guinea pigs or hamsters, may I add that this disease, too, is easily prevented simply by inoculation. If the dog owner has sense, he will get his puppy inoculated against the four evils very quickly indeed, and as soon as the babe approaches his twelfth week the owner should be making an appointment with his local vet to have the dog inoculated. One famous breeder of Border terriers and Jack Russell terriers never had his dogs inoculated, as he stated that inoculation was far too expensive since he kept so many dogs. Sufficient to say, it is false economy to run as many uninoculated dogs. Furthermore, no puppy should go outside its owner's house into the street until it has received its full inoculations, and two weeks after the inoculation is about the correct time to expose a puppy to the disease-ridden world outside the door.

Meanwhile, back in the disease-ridden world we have canicola fever. It is very similar to leptospirosis in symptoms, treatment and, if it goes untreated, the end product, usually death. It is also extremely common, for about 40 per cent of the dogs examined in a Glasgow survey displayed tissue damage caused by canicola fever. Few vets can distinguish the symptoms of this infection from those of leptospiral jaundice without examining blood, faeces and urine samples, so expect almost identical symptoms to the ones described under the heading leptospiral jaundice, or, better still, don't expect such symptoms. Inoculate and prevent the disease from crippling your dog.

It will come as a relief to know we have reached the end of this depressing section about the apocalyptic horsemen of the dog world. Now for a few still unpleasant but eminently curable ailments.

Worms

To speak generally, dogs are troubled with two sorts of worms: roundworms and tapeworms.

Roundworms

These are found, coiled like pieces of wire, in the stomachs of puppies, usually loosely attached to the stomach walls by a beak-like hook. Most are small, a 5-inch worm being a giant, but they infest in such profusion as to cause quite a serious problem. I once wormed a very badly infected puppy aged four months that had been sent up for training from somewhere in the Rhondda. At that time, I was constantly experimenting with anthelmintics (substances which eradicate worms), and dosed the puppy with a chemical called santonin (I'll explain about santonin later). An hour after the dose, the puppy went rigid and began to shake. I confess I panicked and was on the verge of rushing the puppy to the vet. However, in only moments she began to vomit and simultaneously to expel faeces – a whole stool full of worms in fact. Before the hour was out, she had passed eighty-three large adult roundworms.

In spite of the fact that all canines as well as felines are usually plagued by these parasites, there is little reason to believe or accept the current back-to-nature theory that these worms are part and parcel of the canine life-style and do no harm. One idiot I met at the 1974 Game Fair said he believed that worms were put into dogs by the Almighty to prevent dogs becoming fat – a statement scarcely born out by science or by Genesis. Worms have a decidedly harmful effect and one only needs to note the pot-bellies and death-rate in wild dog litters to realize that these parasites are best out of a dog.

There are, of course, many substances that will cause the worm to release its hold on the lining of the dog's stomach and be evacuated, either by vomiting or by passing in the faeces, and modern science has come a considerable way from the time when most dog breeders thrust a cud of chewing tobacco down the throat of the puppy and hoped for the best. This was a common practice when I was a lad, and while it has to be admitted it cleared the puppy of worms, it damned nigh killed the creature into the bargain, and, in fact, many puppies did die through this method. The reader will probably notice I use the word puppy, not adult dog, for an adult dog is rarely troubled with these parasites.

Until a few years ago, a powder called santonin was used to eradicate roundworms in puppies. This powder, made from a plant called *Artemisia maritima*, was produced in Syria and the Lebanon and was a highly effective worming remedy, provided that the stomach and intestines of the puppy were empty, for food seriously interfered with the action of the drug. Thus it was customary to fast the puppies for twenty-four hours before giving the powder. Furthermore, it tended to produce a rather sick puppy when it was used (and the fasting did little good either), so it was unwise to worm puppies under twelve weeks old. Few proprietary worm medicines contain santonin today, however. Incidentally, santonin never had any effect on tapeworms.

Oil of chenopodium, a slimy substance extracted from the Jerusalem oak, is a very useful anthelmintic, and although it passed out of use following the discovery of a new, less toxic chemical called piperazine citrate, it is making a comeback, so to speak, in a newly fashionable herbal worming remedy. If the reader is a 'back-to-nature' addict, may I add that oil of chenopodium is certainly not a mild anthelmintic and has been known to kill cats given it as a vermifuge. It is also not really suitable for sickly puppies and elderly animals, and it has been known to cause pregnant animals to miscarry. Unlike the chemical santonin, oil of chenopodium works best if the puppy has a moderately full stomach, so fasting before administering the drug is unnecessary.

By far the best vermifuge for roundworms is the chemical, piperazine citrate, which is the main component of almost all proprietary modern worm remedies. This chemical offers a safe method of worming puppies, for piperazine citrate is not toxic. Puppies of six weeks old can be wormed with safety, and with no need for fasting. Shaws manufacture a product called Erliworm, which contains piperazine citrate, and this can be given to three-week-old puppies with safety.

A few words of warning, however. Never worm a sick puppy, not even with a mild vermifuge such as piperazine citrate, and do not worm a puppy when worms are leaving the body in number even before the worming medicine is given. The worms are leaving the animal because there is something wrong with the creature – a stomach disturbance, perhaps, or maybe leaving the sinking puppy may explain it rather more cynically. Try to get the puppy well before worming it.

Tapeworms

For some reason, perhaps the great length which they attain, these vile creatures seem to fascinate people, and I confess I am one of them. They certainly fascinate the public health authorities, who literally haunt abattoirs because of these foul parasites, while specimens in jars on display at schools rank high in the interest ratings among children. However, they are no joking matter and can be a serious problem to any dog unlucky to become infected. Tapeworms are long, thin, strip-like creatures that hang suspended in the gut, attached to the wall of the gut by a hooked head-like structure called a scolex. The long, thin tape is made up of several segments, and these are constantly being produced by the scolex until the tapeworm is many feet long. Twenty-two-foot tapeworms are not uncommon at abattoirs and I have seen a 12-foot specimen taken from a dog. Yes, I have to confess, it was my dog. Now, worms of this kind not only absorb food from the host in order to grow, but also, to prevent being digested by the dog as meat would be if suspended in the gut, secrete anti-enzymes that coat the body of the parasite. The amount of food a worm absorbs is negligible, and, anyway, the alimentary canal of a dog is wasteful, so there is food to spare. The real damage is done by this anti-enzyme slime which the worm secretes. It is decidedly toxic and causes inflammation of the gut and great loss of condition in the dog. I have dissected both bovine and rabbit bowels that have held quantities of tapeworms, and in every case the area where the scolex was attached was inflamed. There is no doubt about it: tapeworms will cause a great deal of suffering in a dog.

How to determine if a dog has tapeworms is usually fairly simple. Usually the dog is thin and has what only a stock keeper would understand as 'a bad or staring coat'. The dog may eat ravenously or capriciously, and bad breath is often associated with an infestation.

The most obvious way of determining if a dog is infected, however, is to check his stools. As tapeworm segments become mature, they detach themselves from the main body and become passed with the faeces. Incidentally, the 'ripe' segment contains thousands of fertilized eggs that will in turn grow into other tapeworms if they find a suitable host. Samples of dust taken from around most established kennels usually contain a certain quantity of tapeworm eggs, so it is easy to see how a dog becomes infected. These segments wriggle and convulse awhile, and so anyone who believes his dog to be infected should check the dog's stools daily.

Not only can a dog pick up tapeworms from the dust where other dogs have defaecated, but rabbit entrails are also a rich source of this parasite, for most rabbits are heavily infected. As a matter of interest, one old method of clearing a dog of tapeworms was to boil a rabbit skin and force the dog to eat it. The worms then adhered to the partly digested skin when it was passed in the faeces. Funnily enough, I have found that the method actually works quite well, though it will not totally eradicate worms in a dog. For that one must turn to one of the proprietary worm medicines, and there are many of them.

At the time of writing, one of the most common chemicals used to eradicate worms is Dichlorophen. Unlike the more usual chemicals used as vermifuges – chemicals which stun the worm, causing it to release its grip and be passed in the faeces – Dichlorophen actually removes the protective anti-enzyme layer, allowing the gut to dissolve the tapeworm. Thus no tapeworm or segments will be found in the faeces, though sometimes an offensive, foul-smelling slime is passed, and the only proof one has that the medicine has worked is a rapid improvement in the condition of the dog. This is perhaps the only disadvantage which Dichlorophen has, for it is very rare that a worm is passed whole when this vermifuge is used. Its advantages are that it is non-toxic and has very few after-effects. Furthermore, it does not require that the dog be fasted before dosing. Personally, I do not like this type of worming remedy, since I wish to see the results of the worming, but this is not perhaps scientific reasoning. Veterinary researches have indicated that this is perhaps the most effective anthelmintic for the control of tapeworms.

During my youth, the most popular worming medicines contained areca. This is a natural substance which is simply ground-up betel nuts of the kind chewed by certain Orientals just as we chew chewing gum. These Orientals must remain absolutely clear of parasites such as tapeworm, as areca is very effective in ridding any dogs of worms. The most common dosage of areca nut was to give a dog as much nut as would cover a sixpence – a heaped mound would suffice for a large dog, a thin layer be adequate for a small dog. The dog needed to be starved for twenty-four hours at least before being given the powder, and the results were very rapid. I wormed my first terrier with areca – I was nine at the time – and walked only perhaps a mile before she passed an enormous tapeworm.

Areca nut is rarely sold these days, and has been superseded by a chemical derivative called arecoline acetarsol, which is the active ingredient of such proprietary worm medicines as Tenoban. This chemical is very effective and causes the worm to be expelled whole. As with areca nut, the reaction is very rapid. It is rather a toxic substance, however, and cannot be bought across the counter like most other worm remedies. Vets, however, stock this useful vermifuge. As it is slightly toxic, it should never be given to sickly, aged or pregnant animals.

Extract of male fern is another formerly common anthelmintic, though it is rarely found in modern worming medicines. It is a mixture of two chemicals called filicic acid and aspidinal, made by steeping the rhizomes of male ferns in ether. It is an extremely old vermifuge, and male fern roots were fed to cattle to clean them of worms before Chaucer set about writing *The Canterbury Tales*. It required a lengthy fasting of an animal, up to forty-eight hours not being too long, if it was to be really effective. For this reason, it was not popular, but it does work, and works extremely well. Herbal worming remedies, now becoming very popular at the present time, usually contain male fern extract. Again, I must caution the reader: this extract can be dangerous if given to pregnant bitches or very young puppies.

Skin Infections

Mange

Loosely speaking there are two sorts of mange: *follicular* and *sarcoptic*. For the sake of convenience, we will deal with sarcoptic mange first.

Sarcoptic mange, or scabies, as it is called when it infects humans, is caused by a mite called *Sarcoptes scabiei*, or sometimes by another allied variety, *Sarcoptes communis*, a type more commonly found on foxes and rats than on dogs. The havoc caused by both these mites is horrendous, and not only are they extremely irritating, they are also very debilitating and will reduce an animal to a piteous state in days. Sarcoptic mange usually starts to manifest itself on the muzzle of the dog, and then works backwards. It causes intense itching and drives the dog nearly demented. In next to no time, the dog will be covered in sores caused by scratching to alleviate the itching.

The disease can also be highly communicable to humans, as I know full well, for I contract scabies every time a mange outbreak attacks my dogs. Some people seem remarkably resistant to scabies, while others contract it easily. Skin pigmentation in humans apparently has a lot to do with resistance to scabies, and, funnily enough, long-coated dogs seem remarkably resistant to mange. As I hunt rat regularly, my dogs are literally plagued with mange. During one bad outbreak, when my Jack Russell terriers literally became bald with mange, my Border terriers were totally unaffected in spite of the fact that some were kennelled with the infected Jack Russell terriers. A good piece of advice now: treat the mange as soon as you see it. If it gets a hold on a dog, it will bring untold misery and cause great expense in getting the dog cleared of this hellish disease.

One of the earliest mangicides was flowers of sulphur stirred into boiling fat, lard, axle grease or vaseline, the whole sticky mess then being rubbed into the dog. Nasty, smelly and ugly, but such remedies used to work quite well. Old remedies also recommended using a mixture of sulphur and creosote. The creosote used on the dog's skin, particularly on a skin that has been torn and scratched, is agonizing, and causes the dog great and unnecessary distress. Furthermore, a dog covered in this filthy mess is unhandleable for weeks. Also some dogs are allergic to creosote on their skins, and one or two have apparently died from this treatment.

Liver of sulphur or potassium sulphide is an excellent mange dip, in spite of the fact that it smells of rotten eggs. Most medicated mange dips contain this substance. Sadly, it is difficult to obtain these days, but if one can obtain this priceless chemical, it should be kept in a dry, air-tight tin. Not only does the chemical destroy mange mites, fleas and so on, but once the dog's hair has grown back after a mange attack, it has an excellent sheen. Sulphides are absorbed through the skin, so don't be surprised to find your dog passing somewhat pungent-smelling urine for days after being dipped in liver of sulphur. It is an excellent mangicide, as is selenium sulphide, an allied chemical that is fairly readily obtainable and far more stable than potassium sulphide. Selene is one of the proprietary names for a solution of selenium sulphide.

Just recently, chemicals like Alugan, a complex organic phosphide, have appeared on the market, and it has met with mixed results. Two of my associates praise it, in fact swear by it, but I have not found it particularly effective, possibly because my mange problems are caused by *Sarcoptes communis*, the rat or fox mange. Sufficient to say that this chemical is well worth trying.

Gamma BHC dips – that is, dips containing gamma benzene hexachloride – have proved very efficient in the past, particularly in the control of sheep mange or pig scab caused by *Sarcoptes scabiei*. Provided the maker's instructions are followed precisely, the chemical is usually quite safe, though one or two animals have turned out to be allergic to Gamma BHC and have convulsed after coming into contact with it. Black's quotes one farmer's wife becoming ill after coming into contact with this dip, experiencing convulsions and going into a thrashing fit. I hasten to add that such occurrences are very rare indeed. Up to a few years ago, I had great success with this chemical and was delighted with its results in the treatment of mange. Lately, however, there is some evidence to suggest that many mange mites are becoming resistant to Gamma BHC. If one is hunting rat and fox regularly, then the dogs should be dipped regularly in suspensions of Gamma BHC. This can be costly if one buys mangicides manufactured for dogs, but quite cheap dips can be made by buying sheep dip, or pig mange control dip, for these are usually sold in quite large quantities and are therefore quite inexpensive to buy. Mange is an ever-present problem with my own ratting team, and I dip my dogs immediately after every hunt in a tub containing Gamma BHC. This manages to hold the disease in check, even if it doesn't completely eradicate it.

Another mangicide that has had good results in the treatment of sarcoptic mange is a complex sulphur-based chemical called Tetmosol. This is an extremely poisonous substance, so the maker's instructions must be obeyed to the letter. It is not a suitable mangicide to use on small puppies or ailing dogs, but it is certainly effective in clearing mange. I once cleared a very bad case of ferret mange using this substance, but caution is advised when using Tetmosol. It is not a substance one should use with reckless abandon. I have known dogs convulse and die when their owners have failed to heed the maker's instructions.

Perhaps one of the best all-round mangicides is the good old faithful benzyl benzoate, which is not only effective but extremely cheap, and which used to be used as a treatment for human scabies. Few doctors prescribe benzyl benzoate as a scabicide today, since it causes erythema or reddening of the tissue when applied to the human body, but it is still a highly effective way of controlling the ravages of *Sarcoptes scabiei*. When it comes into contact with scratches it stings, much like iodine, so some dogs which are heavily infested with mange and have scratched themselves often react wildly when treated. Try not to cover all the dog with this emulsion: cover half of the dog on day one and the other half on day two, continuing until the dog is clear of mange. Hair usually takes about six weeks to grow back on an infected dog, so do not expect overnight miracles.

Kennel hygiene is vital if the dog is not to be reinfected with the mite. Straw makes an unsatisfactory sort of bedding for a mange sufferer, since not only does it cause additional itching, it also tends to harbour mange mites. Newspaper makes a useful bedding, and it can be cleaned out and burnt daily. Shavings are even better, and sawdust from creosoted wood is not only an excellent bedding, but its chemical contents deter the mange mite. I used to get sawdust from a yard that specialized in sawing up old pickled railway sleepers, and mange was non-existent in my kennels at the time. Burn all mange-infested bedding, and burn it quickly. About five years ago I composted a load of straw used to bed down my mange sufferers. After five months, I forked out the rotting bedding on to my potato crop, and while I have to admit that I had a fine crop of potatoes, I also have to confess to an equally fine crop of scabies sores as a result of my contact with the bedding. Continue to apply the mangicide long after the scabies pustules have disappeared, and an occasional fumigation of the kennels and scrubbing out with bleach once in a while helps. Many hunt kennels char the woodwork of the hounds' stalls with a blowlamp once in a while, and many still scrub the benches with near-boiling soda solution.

Since mange mites are becoming resistant, even to highly efficient mangicides such as Gamma BHC, frequent attacks with all the chemicals mentioned above often work well. To clear my latest mange outbreak, I used weekly dips of Gamma BHC, coated the dogs with benzyl benzoate daily, and used a selenium sulphide dip once a month. A badly infected dog with many mange sores should be scrubbed with a mild solution of soda before treatment as the soda removes the fatty or oily film that protects the mange mite. Mange can be cured, but it is not easy to achieve. Even after the dog is clear of the infection, weekly dips in Gamma BHC are useful. Above all, never allow young children to play with mangy dogs. I teach in a socially deprived area – they called such a district a slum in my youth, but modern parlance tends to be a little kinder – and many children in the district suffer from scabies. If the Public Health and Child Welfare Group were to dip all the mange-ridden dogs that throng the streets, I feel scabies would become almost unknown in that district.

Follicular mange is a baffling malady, and one which the various veterinary groups should spend much money in investigating. Very little is known about the progress of this unpleasant disorder, and still less about its cure. All that is certain is that it is caused in part by a cigar-shaped mite that lives in the fatty tissue beneath the skin of the dog. Thus it is very difficult to treat this mite, which often denudes the dog of hair completely. Certain strains of dachshund were rendered extinct by their inability to resist the disease, and inability seems the right word. Some time ago I visited a farm near Buxton and saw a dachshund grey-black with mange sharing a basket with a long-haired terrier that was completely free of the infection.

The symptoms of the disease are fairly obvious, though they are inclined to be variable. Frequently the dog's hair simply falls out and the skin looks blue-black, like the hide of an elephant. Unlike sarcoptic mange, which is maddeningly irritating, follicular mange rarely causes itching or irritation of the skin. The skin may, however, be scaly or covered in pus-filled spots.

So much for the symptoms. Treatment is a far different matter. Most methods used to eradicate this disease are not very effective, but, for heaven's sake, try before you take the easy way out and destroy the dog. Medicated dips in sulphurous chemicals have been known to help – sometimes. (I'm afraid 'help sometimes' is the right expression to use for all the chemicals used to treat mange of this type.) It is advisable to keep the dog in the very peak of physical condition to keep follicular mange at bay, and once the dog is known to be susceptible to this malady, any drop in condition, either through teething, illness or even parturition, will produce the symptoms.

Some time ago I had a friend who 'flapped' greyhounds. To the uninitiated, that means raced dogs on unlicensed tracks where the rules are sometimes, to say the least, a bit lax. Now, greyhounds race best and perform fastest when they are at a particular weight. A half-pound over or under that optimum weight produces a dog that is below par regarding its racing time. Many racing men weigh their dogs just prior to a race to gauge the dog's chances of success. My friend had a slightly more macabre method – he would only bet on his greyhound when it manifested the first sign of follicular mange, for he knew that its body fat had by then been fasted off the dog. On the night it was to run at peak condition, it would display just a few elephant-hide-like black patches. Three days later it would look ghastly, and need to be fattened to eradicate the symptoms.

Tonics containing arsenic are often prescribed as a cure, for arsenic in sub-Crippen doses acts as a stimulant. Even then it is still a hit-and-miss affair. Only recently, a firm has produced a herbal treatment for follicular mange, and one American pharmaceutical company is experimenting with a vaccine to curb the effects of the disease. As a squeak of hope from the bottom of my inevitable Pandora's box, some dogs do recover from this unsightly skin complaint.

Eczema

Eczema is another baffling skin complaint, probably caused by an allergy to a specific substance. Some dogs are allergic to fish, others to Agen or nitrogen trichloride, the substance used to bleach flour to produce white bread. They react in peculiar manner, losing hair, sometimes falling into furious fits when fed white bread. Other dogs experience no reaction when fed these same substances. One bitch I knew developed a bad patch of wet eczema when kennelled in wooden buildings, a patch which promptly disappeared immediately she was housed in a concrete kennel. Obviously the malady is not transferable to other dogs, but the tendency to develop such allergies may be inherited. A change of diet will frequently remedy the situation, but, failing this, veterinary treatment should be sought.

Incidentally, a vet who diagnoses eczema instantly without examining a skin scraping from the infected area under a microscope is a little suspect in my book, I'm afraid. It is impossible to distinguish eczema from mange with any certainty without such a skin scraping, and vets who boast they can do so are kidding you and themselves. My own vet, who is a whizz-kid with small animals, always takes skin scrapings when I bring in a dog that has resisted treatment. As soon as the disease is diagnosed as eczema, the vet will usually attempt a variety of treatments in the hope that one will ease the skin disease. Do not regard the vet who does this as incompetent, for this complaint will often need much trial-and-error treatment before a cure can be effected.

Wounds

These, of course, are among the everyday hazards of working a team of terriers, or, indeed, of owning more than one terrier, for terriers are quarrelsome dogs and kennel fights are far from infrequent. A word of advice before kicking off on the treatment of wounds. Kennel three terriers together at your peril. Two will simply fight until a peck order has been established. Three will invariably fight with far more serious repercussions, for while one terrier engages his foe jaw to jaw, the third terrier will invariably latch on to the belly of the antagonist, and gut wounds are not only dangerous, but very often fatal even if given expert veterinary attention. I frequently get people, particularly ladies, who ask my advice on matters concerning their dogs (and rarely take that advice, I should add), and I equally frequently find three or more terriers kennelled together 'like one big happy family', so their owners tell me; but sooner or later tragedy occurs. The great tragedy is that few people will heed the advice of not kennelling two terriers together. I repeat: two will fight to establish a canine order of peck; three will invariably battle to the death.

On the subject of fights, the most savage battles one will usually encounter are usually between babes of four to five months of age. Some of these infantile battles are far from infantile in their ferocity, and skirmishes can continue until both combatants are exhausted. Provided these battles are not three-way events, it is wise to allow them to continue until the question of supremacy is settled. It is, in fact, better to let two youngsters fight it out while you are in a position to watch and prevent serious damage than to kennel them after stopping the fight so that the battle can go on in private. After puppies have attained six or seven months of age, fights are far more rare.

The psychology of such battles is fascinating. In wild dogs, foxes included, battles between youngsters usually establish a law of peck that prevents serious damage to members of a pack at a later date, for any member of a pack that is incapacitated reduces the hunting efficiency of the group. In the case of foxes and other solitary canines, such battles serve to disperse the litters over a wide area, thereby ensuring that the immediate district is not denuded of available game. Man may have domesticated the dog, even altered the canine dietary tract, but various primitive traits are still present in even the family pet to remind us that our dogs are only one step away from their wild ancestors. Puppy fights are usually furious, but are seldom very damaging unless, of course, one of the milk teeth penetrates the abdomen of an adversary.

Enough, however, of kennel fights. Wounds are usual occupational hazards of hunting with terriers. Rat bites are all too frequent in my own team, and though my veterans have developed a fair degree of immunity to the infections introduced by rat bites, youngsters starting the game are not so immune and suffer badly from them. Rat bites should be cleaned carefully with an antiseptic solution and dusted with an antibiotic, if one has access to antibiotic powders. Furthermore, if a rat bite looks like being reluctant to heal, a visit to a vet is essential. Many people avoid treating wounds since they believe in the cleaning action of a dog's saliva as the dog licks his wounds. There is much truth in this, as the saliva of mammals contains a powerful antiseptic called lysozyme – remember the parable of Lazarus who had his sores licked by dogs? But many wounds inflicted by rats are on the muzzle and near the eyes, places where a dog finds it impossible to lick. It is also wise not to overestimate the healing value of the saliva of the dog. Wounds need proper attention for the dog to be fit and well for the next hunt.

Fox bites are veritable devils when it comes to festering, for a fox is a noted filth feeder and its saliva must contain a host of unpleasant bacteria. A dog that has been badly bitten by a fox usually develops a very swollen face, for fox bites are invariably found on a dog's muzzle and head. These need treatment, and not the salt-water treatment advised by all too many hunt servants, but treatment with proprietary antiseptics plus a shot of antibiotics to combat deeper infection. I have known untreated fox bites to take a turn for the worse and the dog to die as a result of septic poisoning. If a dog looks off-colour, off his food and generally low in condition a week after a battle with a fox, get him to a vet without delay. Fox wounds are dangerous, believe me. Don't, I repeat, don't, heed the advice given by a great many amateurs and cauterize the wound by inserting into it a hot knife blade. Your dog may have his wounds rendered free from infection by this method, but he stands a thoroughly good chance of dying of shock after the drastic treatment. The science of antiseptics has progressed a great deal since such methods were the only means available of treating a bad wound.

Badger bites, which are usually found beneath the neck and shoulders of the dog who has been in conflict with a Brock, rarely fester, not because the badger is an infection-free creature, but because of the nature of the wounds. These are pincer bites rather than the deep slashes which a fox usually inflicts on the dog. Even so, such bites should be cleaned, and cleaned thoroughly. After a dog has endured a hard struggle with either a fox or a badger, or, for that matter, been damaged in a serious kennel fight, he should be rugged up and kept warm. Pneumonia carries off far more battlers than does septic poisoning. Tend wounded terriers well and you can expect long and faithful service from them. I worked my old veteran up to the day he died, aged twenty-one, and although his body was a mass of scars, he was rarely laid up for long. When in doubt consult a vet is the dictum the terrier man must always remember.

Ear Canker

This is a far from uncommon complaint, or, rather, symptom, for it is a term applied to a variety of ear infections. Most canker is caused by a tiny mite called the otodectic mite which lives in the outer ear and causes such irritation that some dogs have been driven mad by the itching. Most dogs scratch infected ears, thereby bringing new infection, and the ear reacts to the mite by producing a foul-smelling brown wax. This should be cleaned out with a spirit solution, and a few drops of ear-canker treatment, which usually contains Gamma BHC, then put in the ears. Frequent treatment is required if the mite is to be destroyed. I dip my dogs in a BHC filled vat to check mange, and some of this is bound to get in the ears, so my dogs are rarely troubled with ear canker. Last year, however, my stud dog, Vampire, contracted the malady, and in spite of dips and daily treatment I failed to exterminate the mite. Complex aural surgery was needed to clean out the ears of the infection the mite had introduced, and, I should add, it was expensive surgery at that. Ears should be checked daily, particularly those of a dog that works rats or goes to ground, for soil and filth are great breeding grounds for the otodectic mite.

Fleas and Ticks

Fleas and ticks are the final occupational hazards of the working terrier, but are easily cured. Dips which kill or prevent mange mites will also make conditions fairly hectic for fleas and ticks. Don't play around with ticks, pulling them off the dog, burning them to make them release their hold, and so on. A tick that dies leaving the sucking headpiece still in the dog is a nuisance, since the head invariably causes sepsis and inflammation. Dip infected dogs in Gamma BHC or liver of sulphur solution and the ticks will simply become torpid and fall off. Dogs which are allowed to run in sheep pasture invariably become infested with ticks, and badger-digging dogs are also victims of these unpleasant blood-sucking insects.

A powerful jaw is a prime requisite of a working terrier: the author's champion Warlock.

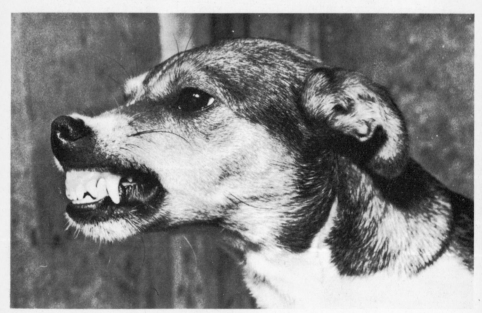

A correct scissor bite. See standard of excellence for the Jack Russell Terrier.

APPENDIX

The Jack Russell Terrier Club of Great Britain
PRESIDENT: JIMMY EDWARDS ESQ.

Aims: The Central Committee has formulated the accompanying standard to achieve a uniform type of Jack Russell terrier; and by means of shows, teach-ins, discussions and the formation of branches in all counties, eventually it is hoped to educate the breeders and the lay public as to the correct type.

PROVISIONAL STANDARD, *compiled January 1975*

Height: To allow for the different sizes in Jack Russell terriers, two heights are allowed: up to 15 inches at the shoulder; and 11 inches and under at the shoulder, to allow for the small type.

Head: Strong-boned head with powerful jaws and good strong cheek muscles. Dark, almond-shaped eyes with well-pigmented rims and a good pigment on the nose. Small V-shaped, dropped ears carried close to the head. (When viewed from the front, the fold of the ears will be slightly above the crown of the skull.)

Teeth: The points of the upper incisors slightly overlapping the lower.

Body: Straight back, with high-set tail, at least 4 inches long and carried gaily. The front of the body should be well muscled with strong shoulders on straight front legs. The chest should be able to be spanned by two hands behind the shoulder blades. The rear must be well put together, strong muscle and good angulation. Feet, cat-like, with unsightly dew claws removed.

Coat: Smooth or broken coated (no long woolly coats).

Colour: Basically white, with tan, tricolour or traditional hound markings, including ticked and mottled.

Undesirable characteristics (any of these features would render a terrier ineligible for the Advanced Register – see below): Characteristics of alien breeds, i.e. Sealyham, bull terrier, wire fox terriers, Lakelands, etc., pricked ears, crooked front legs, brindle markings, putty noses, unpigmented eye-rims, curly tails.

Registration: All terriers belonging to club members can be registered on the Foundation Register. However, if an owner considers his dog or bitch of sufficient merit, it can be presented to one of the regional inspectors for personal examination; if the inspector considers the animal of sufficient merit to perpetuate the breed, and that it shows no outward sign of hereditary defects, the dog will be entered in the élite ADVANCED REGISTER.

NOTE: The terrier must be at least 15 months of age, and previously entered in the Foundation Register, as above.